FROM AN OFFICE BUILDING WITH A HIGH-POWERED RIFLE

A REPORT TO THE PUBLIC FROM AN FBI AGENT INVOLVED IN THE OFFICIAL JFK ASSASSINATION INVESTIGATION

DON ADAMS

From an Office Building with a High-Powered Rifle: A Report to the Public from an FBI Agent Involved in the Official JFK Assassination Investigation

Copyright © 2012 Don Adams All Rights Reserved.
Editor: Jody Miller

Published by:
TrineDay LLC
PO Box 577
Walterville, OR 97489
1-800-556-2012
www.TrineDay.com

Library of Congress Control Number: 2012936844

Adams, Don — Author
From an Office Building with a High-powered rifle: A Report to the Public from an FBI Agent Involved in the Official JFK Assassination Investigation—1st ed.
p. cm.
Epub (ISBN-13) 978-1-936296-87-3
Mobi (ISBN-13) 978-1-936296-88-0
Print (ISBN-13) 978-1-936296-86-6
1. Kennedy, John F. -- (John Fitzgerald), -- 1917-1963 -- Assassination. 2. Conspiracies -- United States -- History -- 20th century. 3. Adams, Don. 4. United States. -- Federal Bureau of Investigation -- Officials and employees -- Biography. I. Adams, Don . II. Title

First Edition
10 9 8 7 6 5 4 3 2 1

Printed in the USA
Distribution to the Trade by:
Independent Publishers Group (IPG)
814 North Franklin Street
Chicago, Illinois 60610
312.337.0747
www.ipgbook.com

Publisher's Foreword

Forgive your enemies, but never forget their names.

– John F. Kennedy

Growing up in the 1960s meant many things: the most profound, the most traumatic, the most shocking, the most interesting, the most melancholy, the ugliest … was the brutal killing of our leaders. First, there was our president, a virile scion ensconced in Camelot, then five years later, America's most successful practitioner of Gandhi's non-violent political change stratagem and then to cap off the trifecta spree – the slain president's younger brother.

I had recently turned fourteen when JFK was killed and long on eighteen when his brother Bobby was shot – talk about some bloody bookends for the adolescent years. The assassinations altered my life. When they happened, I felt shock, anger, sadness, and bewilderment, but as the saying says, "Life goes on."

Later, I knew something was deeply wrong, especially starting in late 1969, after my ex-spook father told me some things I didn't quite comprehend.

I knew there was something happening, way beyond the simple breaking of commandments, but what exactly was amiss I didn't have a clue. Years of study, book learning and discussions have brought about a keener appreciation of our predicament, and I am always delighted to find a story with honor that furthers our knowledge of any of these grave red-raw crucibles of our times.

Don Adams is a remarkable man, and his personal story of integrity shows without any doubt: conspiracy, collusion and confusion surround the very public murder of the 35th President of the United States.

From an Office Building with a High-Powered Rifle: A Report to the Public from an FBI Agent Involved in the Official JFK Assassination Investigation is Don Adam's exclusive chronicle of his front-seat view of the probe, with a unique look at one of the most intriguing pieces of the JFK assassination collage: Joseph Adams Milteer.

Milteer and his *words* have piqued the interests of conspiracy researchers, ever since the first inklings came out in Miami in early 1967 about "a 'tape' which was made two or three weeks prior to the assassination of President Kennedy predicting the President's assassination."

Well, Milteer did "predict" the murder – under any definition of the term. But as Adams declares, "He was hardly a prophet, but just how involved he really was, we may never know."

There is much to learn from Adams' story: connivance, deceit, and distortion by federal officials both before and after the assassination to deflect inquiry from its natural course and affect its outcome. And there is something there … there.

Somehow, some way, Milteer, I believe, *knew*: through the shadowy threads that bind the abyss of military, government and social/economic espionage. A menagerie of competing interests that many times employ the same double/triple/quadruple agents: Creations, who have no idea whose water they are carrying and what the whole shebang is really about.

No way to run a railroad … or a country. *From an Office Building with a High-Powered Rifle* gives us a powerful opportunity to understand part of our shaded past, helping us stand up to the rigors of the present, and meet the demanding challenges of the future.

We should – for our children's sake, for the world's sake, for … our sake – take our country back. Back from the darkness of despair, striving forward to the boon of responsible governance, honest relationships and a real tomorrow.

Onwards to the utmost of Futures!

Peace,
Kris Millegan
Publisher
TrineDay
May 1, 2012

Table of Contents

Special Acknowledgement

The author wrote this book with three main goals. First, that the writings must be as truthful as possible. Second, to mesh the writings with information that was obtained from caring contributors, archives, magazines, newspapers, books and other sources. The author is pleased to say he believes that this has been accomplished.

A third requirement was to have a good publisher to produce the book. After reading many of the chapters in preparation of the published book, the author says, "I must say that I am overly pleased with what I have read. It's excellent."

Kris Millegan Publisher, and Kelly Ray, Editor of Trine-Day have done a most professional job in filling those three goals and I believe that the purchasers of the book will agree with the author. The author could not have chosen better persons to hold their titles. They are truly the best Publisher and Editor. I have spent most of my time working with Kris and we have become a good solid team and good friends. We are all fortunate to have this team working together.

Donald Adams, Author

Dedication and Appreciation

"I am only as important as one grain of sand in all the beaches of the world."
– Donald A. Adams

I dedicate this book to God, who made us what we are and gave us the talents to be what He wanted us to be. I am what God made me. Without His gifts of heavenly wisdom, common sense and faith, all of my accomplishments would not have been possible. I know that He is with me each moment of the day and night. Because of this, I do not fear.

I thank the Good Lord with all my being for his being so generous to me and for letting me love law enforcement as I do. He has charted the road I travel, leading from the past to the present and the writing of my story.

None of this would have been possible without the total support of my wife Jeanette. Without her willingness to stay by my side when I changed careers and became an agent with the FBI and without her numerous sacrifices throughout all of these 57 years, I couldn't have fulfilled my dream. She went through very trying times – packing, moving eight times in ten years, and caring for the children in my absence. Included in that mix were the four serious illnesses of three of our children and me, some with lifetime effects. I know it's not been easy, and I love and appreciate her with all of my heart for being the wife of my life.

My recognition and appreciation must also go to my four children Jeff, and his wife Laura; Dawn; Mark, and his wife Terrie; and Doug and his wife Michele. Doug and Michele were the first in the family to encourage me to tell the story that needed to be told. They had a professional company videotape my "Kennedy Assassination" presentation. They also named their daughter "Kennedy" because they love the name, but also because of my deep involvement with the Kennedy assassination. No one could have done something more meaningful than that for me. I have never had anyone love me like Kennedy and her sister, Kolby, do. I'm a very lucky guy.

My grandson, Jason, and his fiancée Amanda spent considerable time with me to help purchase my laptop on which these writings have been done. Jason also put in long hours teaching me how to use the computer, and his mom, Gwen, was always there for me, as well. My family's support was the foundation for my being able to write my story.

Jeanette and I now have 11 grandchildren and a foster grandchild, and they were all very supportive of me and my work. I thank Jason, Michael, Jonathan, twins Matthew and Melissa, Benny, twins Vincent and Vallerie, Carmine, Kennedy, Kolby and Jillian.

Jason and Amanda Adams recently announced the birth of great grand-daughter Siena Marie Adams.

I truly love my family very deeply.

I want to acknowledge a number of other persons who were in some way involved in support and encouragement to get me started and then to continue until the book was completed. With apologies for forgetting anyone, I'll start with Tim Hanna and Abe Zaiden, both of whom who were the very first to say "Don, write your book."

When I worked as Chief of Police in Fairlawn, a young lady came to my office after reading a newspaper article about me. Deanie Richards spent every free minute working on the Kennedy assassination, and she has been instrumental in providing me with copies of numerous documents. I owe her more than I can say because the material she gave me helped to tell my story.

I need to thank special friends, Dr. Jeff Caufield and Andy Kiel. The three of us have spent a lot of hours together. Jeff is in the process of writing his own book on the JFK assassination. Andy teaches history at Wooster High School in Wooster, Ohio and has invited me to talk with a number of his graduating classes. He is also the author of the book, "J. Edgar Hoover, The Father of the Cold War." Both Jeff and Andy have given solid information to assist me in areas that I knew nothing about and for which I am most grateful.

Tim Hanna and I have been close friends for more than 25 years, and we talked a lot about my involvement with Joseph Adams Milteer. It was Tim who suggested and then went with me to the National Archives in Washington D.C. and College Park, Maryland, to obtain documents for review. That was the best action we could have taken. I owe Tim much appreciation, and this book is a part of him.

Martha Murphy of the National Archives made our time there very productive. She pulled four carts of document folders in which we found a number of vital documents to better illustrate and confirm my suspicions.

In talking about contacts, there are friends that have, in one way or another, been inspirational and supportive to me because of the people they are. Among those friends, I must mention George Fellows, Earl Sumner, Bob McGuiness, Jim Rogers, Art Ryall, Pete Norregard, Tony DeLuca, Jim McCready and Cypress Co. friends. I can't forget all of the law enforcement officers whose lives have touched and influenced mine. Also, I thank Hank Polombo, Jim Huntsman, Jim Honsberger, Dale and Mary Jean Leonhardt. Ben Harrison, Larry Dannemiller, Tom Dannemiller Jr., Wendy Sawyer, Jim Albanese and Donna Kline. Thanks to Ted and Pat Varga for their help with the DVDs. Also a special thanks to friend Paul Waickman who provided me with numerous books about President Kennedy and the FBI. Ann Brennan for the very nice office that I have in my home. Bill Aylward is a very special of many years.

I cannot forget to thank Father William Karg, Fr. John Valencheck, Fr. Matthew Pfeiffer, and Deacon Terry Peacock. Their guidance and inspiration helped me through the rough times.

Finally, I thank very special friend, Jody Miller. The second time was the charm when I asked her to edit my book. I had been writing it since 1997, and it was more than 12 years later that her agreement to help me took a huge load off of my mind. She and I became an excellent working team, and she was able to take all of my voluminous written material and squeeze it down like a tube of tooth paste at its end. Thank you, Jody.

Donald A. Adams
June 2011

Fabian Bachrach

INTRODUCTION

The murder of President John F. Kennedy on the 22nd of November 1963 has been documented, researched and commented upon more than any single historical event in the 20th century. The killing of both JFK and Lee Harvey Oswald was captured live on film. Yet, half a century later, there is still no consensus on who murdered JFK, and why. Myriad questions remain unanswered, and hundreds of theories abound.

As a rookie FBI Agent I played a small part in that epic drama, and the story I have to tell sheds new light on the roles that persons within that agency played in muddying the waters and compromising the investigations, both before and after the crime.

This work has been most difficult for me. During the last two decades I have been investigating actions by the very agency at which I spent 20 years and for which I still have the greatest respect. I love the FBI, and always will. The vast majority of men and women who serve in it are dedicated to this country and its Constitution. They are persons of the very highest standards, and their work reflects a solid foundation of values and principals. That is what makes the FBI the greatest law enforcement agency in the business. I am very proud to have been part of it.

Unfortunately, over the years since my retirement from the Bureau, my subsequent private investigations and document studies have resulted in the discovery of inconsistencies, discrepancies, and outright forgeries. I have learned that crucial information was withheld from me as an agent investigating a planned assassination of the president, just weeks before it actually took place. These documents are in the public record, so I am not breaching anyone's confidentiality rights. Everyone who knows me knows that I tell it like it is. From the perspective of hindsight, maybe I should have sounded the alarm many years ago, but I think a combination of inexperience and idealism blinded me at the time. I have to admit that the desire to keep my brand new job and to have a successful career was a major factor as well. What I write here is the truth to the best of my knowledge and memory. I lived it, and I am convinced that the official investigation was purposely compromised, and, even worse, that the assassination itself could have been prevented.

Both the Secret Service and the FBI had prior warnings. They were in possession of a taped conversation from Nov. 9, 1963 concerning a plan to shoot the president with a high-powered rifle from an office building. Both agencies also received specific information that this could happen in Dallas on November 22nd. Yet, less than two weeks later, the president was permitted to ride in an open car, at five miles per hour, through Dallas streets towered over by tall buildings.

The depth of planning that would have been required to set in motion and to implement all aspects of the assassination would have to have been unprecedented. That planning would have involved people either "in" on the assassination; or those duped by people in positions of power; or those afraid to act on their own, outside of normal protocol; those unwilling to question authority; or those neglecting to follow the rules of procedure in any investigation, let alone the assassination of a president of the United States. There could also have been a "perfect storm" of events that transpired to conceal the truth of what really happened.

I have come to believe that the FBI's investigation was compromised from the top down, beginning with FBI Director J. Edgar Hoover. His authority at that time was unquestioned, and his prerogative to direct the focus of any investigation was sacrosanct. The investigation of any criminal act begins with the basic facts. Those facts build the case. No clues or evidence should be ignored, altered, destroyed, hidden, and most especially, falsified. If any of that occurs, the investigation is flawed, compromised, and becomes "garbage" law enforcement. When the leader of a law enforcement agency, or any hierarchical organization, sets high ethical standards and maintains them, those standards will be reflected in the group as a whole. However, if that leader lets those values weaken due to political or ideological considerations, this will also be reflected in the behavior of underlings. This, I believe, is what happened with Hoover and the FBI before, during and after the assassination of President Kennedy. The question is, how many persons inside and outside the Bureau were affected by this slide into corruption, and what effect did that have on the truthfulness of the investigation?

Justice is defined as "the principal of moral rightness; equity" or "the upholding of what is just, especially, fair treatment and due reward in accordance to honor, standards, or law; fairness." Justice was not served in this case; it was thrown in a dark closet and forgotten. I don't think that is why the statue of Justice in front of the Supreme Court Building is blindfolded. It is my hope that this story will provide a new piece in the giant jigsaw puzzle, and re-open some questions with regard to how this great tragedy was allowed to happen, and then so shoddily (and shadily) investigated.

Donald A. Adams
April 2012

Joseph A. Milteer

TRANSCRIPT OF MILTEER-SOMERSETT TAPE

This is partial transcript of a tape recording from Nov 9, 1963 of Miami Police informant William Somersett having a conversation with right-wing extremist Joseph A. Milteer.

SOMERSETT: I don't know, I think Kennedy is coming here on the 18th, or something like that to make some kind of speech, I don't know what it is, but I imagine it will be on the TV, and you can be on the look for that, I think it is the 18th that he is suppose to be here. I don't know what it is suppose to be about.

MILTEER: You can bet your bottom dollar he is going to have a lot to say about the Cubans, there are so many of them here.

SOMERSETT: Yeah, well he will have a thousand bodyguards, don't worry about that.

MILTEER: The more bodyguards he has, the easier it is to get him.

SOMERSETT: What?

MILTEER: The more bodyguards he has the more easier it is to get him.

SOMERSETT: Well how in the hell do you figure would be the best way to get him?

MILTEER: *From an office building with a high-powered rifle*, how many people [room noise--tape not legible] does he have going around who look just like him? Do you know about that?

SOMERSETT: No, I never heard that he had anybody.

MILTEER: He has got them.

SOMERSETT: He has?

MILTEER: He has about fifteen. Whenever he goes any place they [not legible] he knows he is a marked man.

SOMERSETT: You think he knows he is a marked man?

MILTEER: Sure he does.

SOMERSETT: They are really going to try to kill him?

Assassination Day

It was just after lunch on Friday, Nov. 22, 1963. Senior Resident Agent Royal McGraw and I were traveling in the Bureau car when a call came out to us with a prearranged code number instructing us to proceed to the Thomasville Highway Patrol Post as quickly as possible. All law enforcement vehicles in Georgia, with the possible exception of the U.S. Secret Service, were equipped with radios having a common band frequency. That meant no conversations were private, and the code number indicated the information they had for us could not be put out over the air.

I remember it was hot that day, especially for November, so the car windows were rolled down. At one point, we stopped at an intersection en route to the Highway Patrol office. A man in the car next to us, who was sitting in the passenger seat, said to McGraw, "Did you hear? The president's been shot!"

You can imagine my shock when I heard those words. My first thought was whether Joseph Adams Milteer of Quitman, Georgia had been involved. I had been sent to investigate him a week earlier. Had I failed to prevent this from happening?

We made our way to the patrol post, and the desk sergeant asked if I was Agent Adams. Although he knew McGraw, the sergeant and I had never met. I showed him my identification, and he told me to go to the Department of Agriculture Office in the Federal Building, where there was an important teletype message for me. In those days, the small Thomasville FBI office did not have teletype capability; however, because of its nationwide reach, the Department of Agriculture did. Whatever information was waiting for me, the office did not want it widely broadcast.

The sergeant repeated what we had already heard: President Kennedy had been shot in Dallas, but said he knew nothing further. Again, I couldn't help but wonder if Milteer was part of the shooting.

Once at the Agriculture Office, I identified myself for the second time and showed my credentials. In the teletype room, the message for me read, "Agent Adams, The President is dead. Call the Atlanta Office immediately."

McGraw and I left and went to our Resident Agency where I called Special Agent in Charge James McMahon in Atlanta. He confirmed that President Kennedy had been assassinated in Dallas a short while earlier. He added that the Agent in Charge of the Secret Service requested that I locate Milteer immediately, interview and then hold him for the Secret Service.

At this point, McMahon got very specific with me about my interview with Milteer. He cautioned me that the interview had to be done carefully and that he was going to instruct me as to the questions I should ask. He added that I was to ask nothing more.

Puzzled by these instructions, I responded that this would be a perfect opportunity to probe Milteer deeply and maybe learn something that would help us solve the assassination. McMahon doggedly repeated that he would provide me five questions and that I was to ask nothing else. I insisted that we needed to use the opportunity to ask Milteer about whom he was in contact with, all the organizations he was connected to, where he had been traveling and anything else I could think of. I was confident that Milteer would make a mistake and tell us something he didn't want us to know. I was also convinced this was an opportunity we might never have again.

My arguments fell on deaf ears.

McMahon became upset with my persistence and was emphatic about the severely limited line of questioning I was to pursue. This struck me as strange at the time, and it never happened again during my entire career with the Bureau. I voiced my concern one more time, and McMahon angrily insisted that

I was to obtain descriptive data on Milteer and then ask only the five questions he had dictated, "You will do as I say and do nothing more." Period. End of discussion.

I was still troubled by his orders, but I knew my boundaries.

It was early afternoon on that Friday when I left for Quitman. I met first with Chief William Elliott and worked with him to locate and detain Milteer. Together, we checked Milteer's residence in Quitman, then his girlfriend C.C. Cofield's residence in Valdosta, about 20 miles away. Milteer was nowhere to be found, nor was Cofield's VW bus that Milteer often drove. In Valdosta, we met with the Sheriff and checked the entire general area, along with specific places frequented by Milteer. Later that evening, we rechecked both houses. There was still no sign of Milteer, so I returned home to Thomasville.

During the search for Milteer that afternoon, I learned that Lee Harvey Oswald had been arrested and charged with killing President Kennedy. That news relieved my mind because I had feared the President was dead because of something I had failed to do in my recent investigation of Milteer.

Don Adams' father guarding JFK, Akron – 1959.

CHAPTER ONE

Dream Fulfilled

In the summer of 1945 I was 14 years old and my dad, a detective with the Akron, Ohio Police Department, took me to the dedication ceremony of a new police pistol range in memory of Clarence Chance, a Cuyahoga Falls police officer killed in the line of duty. The ceremony included a shooting demonstration by two FBI agents, Ken Howe and Chet Willet, from the Akron FBI office. I remember them as tall and slender men, dressed in suits, white shirts and ties, with brimmed hats.

When they finished their demonstration, I was so impressed that I told my dad, "That's what I want to be, an FBI agent."

From that moment on, that's all I thought about, but it took me nearly 20 years to finally reach my FBI "enter on duty" date of Sept. 10, 1962. In the interim, I had graduated from high school, started and dropped out of college, enlisted and spent four years in the army, served in the Korean "Police Action," and fortunately came home in one piece. I proposed to and married Jeanette, and we were blessed to have three children, Jeff, Dawn and Mark. I went back to college and graduated from Kent State University. After a stint as a sales agent for a life insurance company, 18 years after that original career dream, I applied to the Federal Bureau of Investigation at the age of 32.

When I applied to become a special agent, I was 6 feet, 7 inches tall and weighed 287 pounds, so my size posed a nearly impossible obstacle. The Bureau had a weight chart that didn't take into consideration my large frame and heavy bone structure. According to that chart, my height required me to weigh 224 pounds, so I would have to lose more than 60 pounds.

I was determined to lose that weight and immediately went on a tomato and steak diet; I got permission to work out with a local football team during their spring practice and after three months, I weighed 224 pounds; but a final weight and height measurement was required by the FBI and I was measured at 6 feet, 6-3/4 inches. That quarter-inch difference meant I needed to lose another 8 pounds, so I continued my diet and workouts. It took another month, but I lowered my weight to 214 pounds, losing more than 70 pounds in four months!

Once my weight was verified, the Bureau's wheels went into motion. Soon, I received a Western Union message sent to the office in Akron and was excited to read that I was being offered an appointment as a Special Agent of the Federal Bureau of Investigation. This was one of the proudest moments of my life.

The one person I couldn't wait to tell was my dad, but his reaction to my news was more typical of our real relationship. On the surface, dad and I appeared to be close, both as father and son and as friends. But there were two faces to my dad. He and my mother had been divorced before my twin brother and I were born. I admired the work he did as a detective, but I had experienced his inflexibility and his toughness, especially when he didn't get his way. He was strong-willed, never forgot a slight and he believed firmly in the adage that "payback is hell."

I had never told dad about my application to the Bureau. Maybe I didn't want him to be disappointed if I failed, but even more, I was determined to do this on my own. I had even asked the local FBI agents who knew and/or were friends of dad's to keep my application in confidence, so when I got the news, I headed over to the Akron Police Department to find him.

Dad was then the secretary to the chief of police, and he was at his desk. He was surprised to see me, and we chatted until I told him I had something to show him. I handed the telegram to him, thinking he would be pleased and proud.

"What the hell does this mean?" he asked after reading it.

"It means what it says," I responded.

He blew up, and all hell broke loose. I was 32 years old and had achieved my life-long dream, but my dad acted as though I were a teenager who had disappointed him, yet again.

"Do you know how embarrassing this is to me?" he finally asked.

He explained that Cartha "Deke" DeLoach, an assistant to FBI Director J. Edgar Hoover, was a close friend of his. Not knowing that his own son was applying to the Bureau, when he could have helped to ease my entrance to the agency, was more important than my having accomplished admittance to the FBI on my own.

Cartha (Deke) DeLoach

Suddenly, Police Chief Harry Whiddon walked in, smiled, said hello to me and shook my hand. To my surprise, dad did an about face, flashed a big smile and handed the telegram to the Chief.

"This is our surprise to you," I remember my dad saying. "What do you think?"

Chief Whiddon read the telegram and said he was very happy for me. He then asked us to come into his office where he reached for the phone to call Deke in Washington. By what I could overhear of Chief Whiddon's side of the conversation, I realized Deke didn't know that I had received an appointment. After the chief finished talking with Deke, he handed the phone to dad, who pretended he had known all along that I was applying to the FBI, but didn't want to dampen my desire by interfering and calling an "old friend" for help.

You could have knocked me over with a feather when I heard my dad say this after what he and I had just gone through, but I kept my mouth shut. Dad turned the phone over to me, and Deke remarked about my trying to "fool dad" and how that hadn't worked because "you just can't fool your father."

Deke talked about what a "grand guy" my father was and how dad had played a big role in helping him to start his climb up the ladder in the Bureau. Deke then told me that when I got to Washington, I should tell my instructor that I was to go to the Department of Justice and see Assistant Director Deke DeLoach immediately.

That was something I didn't want to hear. I didn't want my father or his friend to be involved in my career at the FBI. It was important to me that I do this on my own merits, however it turned out. When the conversation concluded, I wanted to get away from my dad as fast as possible. I was angry at his initial reaction to my news and hurt that he lied to both Chief Whiddon and Deke to make himself look good at my expense. What he did took a great deal of the pleasure out of my accomplishment.

I arrived in Washington, D.C. a week before my "enter on duty" date of Sept. 10, 1962 for training at the FBI National Academy.

The Academy was the pre-eminent training ground for high-ranking police officers in law enforcement agencies throughout the world. During the 14 weeks of instruction, trainees are immersed in all the different arenas of law enforcement, from firearms training and investigative techniques to forensics and civil and criminal law. The graduates are a close-knit group, and their fraternity is recognized everywhere in the world.

When I entered on duty with the FBI in September 1962, I was called into Assistant Director John Malone's office. Malone was in charge of all training for the FBI, both in Quantico, Va., and in Washington, D.C. He told me that he had singled me out because, at 32, I was some seven years older than the other new agents.

"Do you feel that your age will make it difficult for you because of all the classroom work?"

"If I didn't know I could handle the classroom work, I would never have applied to be an agent in the FBI," I replied.

"That's an excellent answer," Malone said, and he shook my hand and told me to go back to my classroom. I never heard anything about my age after that.

The demands on each new agent were heavy, both in and out of the classroom. We attended about half of our classes at the Old Post Office in Washington, D.C. The other half of our training took place at the Marine base in Quantico, Va., where the FBI National Academy buildings and firing ranges were located. We were taught the Bureau requirements for handling investigations, writing reports and everything in between. There was great emphasis on the Bureau's rigid protocol, and no leeway was allowed in the reporting of investigative results. There were also strict rules on deadlines, and they could not be missed.

We were taught that the case agent was responsible for every aspect of an investigation, and failure to perform to the standards expected could result in reprimand and even dismissal from the service. In addition, the personal conduct of each agent – whether on duty or off – was carefully scrutinized during the entire 14 weeks, and actions could be taken against an agent for conduct not acceptable to the Bureau. We were indoctrinated in those standards, which Director Hoover had established and expected to be followed in all cases.

In Washington, D.C., most of our training consisted of learning the Federal laws and statutes under which we would be working during our FBI careers. This was not easy material, and, between class work and study, there was little spare time left for agents-in-training. In addition, we worked in the field with Washington Field Office agents on a few cases. I recall working a kidnapping case where a baby had been taken out of a local hospital by a female stranger. I accompanied the assigned agent to different places as he tracked down leads in the case. I remember going with him to the D.C. jail and interviewing a subject who insisted he had information about the kidnapping. It turned out he was a female impersonator who just wanted to get out of jail for a while. I learned a great deal from this agent as I studied his moves and how he worked the case.

We also had class at Quantico, and in addition to the Federal laws we needed to know, we received instruction using actual cases as examples. Those cases included everything we would have to investigate, from sex crimes, bank robberies and kidnappings to crimes on government reservations, such as Quantico, thefts and transportation across state lines of property, people and vehicles, and much more.

We had specialized training in driving at high speeds and how to execute various maneuvers. We learned how to enter a building to locate fugitives, and we had extensive firearms training, including the Bureau's way of firing a weapon. This was the only problem I had with FBI standard operating procedure. I used to go to the Akron police firing range and shoot for hours with my dad, and his way was ingrained in me by the time I got to Quantico. Rule number one was speed. He taught me to pull a weapon in one swift movement, go into a crouched position at the same time to make a smaller target, and belly-point the gun.

"Getting a high score at the range doesn't mean a thing when you're dead," he would repeat and repeat.

At Quantico, with the entire class of 50 agents in line facing their respective targets, it became glaringly obvious that I could beat almost everybody in pulling and shooting my weapon. I well remember George Zeiss and other instructors screaming over the loudspeaker, "Adams, what are you doing?"

I heard that so many times during training that I finally learned the Bureau's way. But after I left the Academy for my first assignment, I went back to dad's familiar and effective style.

The training was thorough and, to my mind, outstanding. Director Hoover established hundreds of rules and standard operating procedures – all designed to keep "his" agents safe and consistent. Among those rules and procedures, two stood out for me. One was that when you went out to make an arrest, always take more men than you may actually need. Secondly, take more firepower than you think you need. Doing this may save the life of your fellow agent, an accompanying officer or yourself.

While I was in training, our class had the opportunity to attend one of the FBI graduation ceremonies in downtown Washington. I was the first in our class alphabetically, and when we arrived, I was instructed to take one of the front-row seats, which meant I had a clear view the proceedings. On the stage to the right of the rostrum, President John F. Kennedy, the principal speaker, was seated. Next to him was his brother, Attorney General Robert Kennedy. On the other side of the rostrum was a long table with the diplomas stacked on top. Behind the table, FBI Director Hoover was seated, and directly behind him was Associate Director Clyde Tolson, then another four Bureau officials behind him.

Down on the floor, I observed that every time Director Hoover stood up, Tolson and the other assistants did the same; when Hoover sat down the others dutifully followed suit. It reminded me of "musical chairs," or perhaps the court of a supreme dictator.

Meanwhile, Deke DeLoach was carrying messages in and out. He would hand it to the assistant director sitting at the back of the stage, who would then hand it over the shoulder of the man in front of him, who would hand it over the shoulder of the next man, until the note finally reached Hoover. The Director would read the note, then turn and speak to Tolson, who then turned to the assistant director behind him, and on this went until the reply got back to Deke. He would leave, return with another note, and the ritual would begin again. I remember thinking there was no question that Hoover was the Patriarch and everybody was deferential to him. I was struck by the routine protocol and how rigidly it was followed.

It was common knowledge at the time that when Bobby Kennedy became the U.S. Attorney General, he instituted a number of changes that made Director Hoover furious. One had to do with a button in Hoover's office, which was connected to a buzzer in the offices of the attorneys general. Reportedly, he would press the button and a little while later the summoned attorney general would humbly appear in Hoover's office. When Bobby Kennedy moved into the Department of Justice Building, which housed the offices of the Justice Department and the FBI, he supposedly reversed the process. He would press the button whenever he had something to say to Hoover, requiring the Director to walk to him – a not too subtle and very clear message that there was a new boss in town.

Another test of wills between Hoover and Bobby Kennedy occurred regarding the FBI dress code. Hoover insisted that agents dress in white shirts, ties and suit coats, especially when in the Justice Building. One day, Kennedy called a meeting to discuss his desire to move against organized crime. A number of agents who worked the mob in the big cities, such as New

York, Philadelphia, etc., were invited to attend. When the agents arrived for the meeting, Kennedy suggested the men take off their coats, loosen their ties and roll up their sleeves to be more comfortable. When Director Hoover walked in unannounced and saw the agents in their shirts with ties pulled down and sleeves rolled up, he told them to get up and leave the meeting room immediately. Word was that he was furious and let the U.S. Attorney General know that as FBI director, he, J. Edgar Hoover, would tell his agents how to dress.

Armed with the knowledge of the fractious relationship between Bobby Kennedy and Director Hoover, I started watching for signs of discord. It didn't take long for that discord to become evident.

After President Kennedy's address to the graduates, it was time to present the diplomas. Attorney General Kennedy positioned himself in front of the table to hand out the diplomas; standing behind the table was Director Hoover, who was to place each diploma in the outstretched, open hand of the attorney general. I watched the first few graduates shake hands with President Kennedy and continue down the line to receive their diplomas, when something caught my eye. As the attorney general reached his open hand back to take a diploma, I saw Director Hoover slap it vigorously into Kennedy's hand. He seemed to

increase the velocity with each succeeding slap. I then started to watch Hoover's face, and what I saw surprised me – thinly suppressed anger and an unyielding determination to put everything he could into the snap of the diploma into Kennedy's open palm. I knew then that there was real hatred for the attorney general on the part of the director of the FBI. As events unfolded in the next few years, I often wondered how great a role this animosity played in the subsequent investigation of the assassination of the attorney general's brother.

CHAPTER TWO

Personal Roots

I remember a night when I was about 9 years old, spending the summer at Gram and Gramps' place with my dad. I was in awe of my dad. He was a dignified-looking gentleman, always impeccably dressed and well liked. But to me, the most impressive thing about him was that he was a detective. That was probably why I developed such a love of police work and a deep respect for police officers.

Dad

Dad and mom were divorced, and he lived with his parents. These summers were special; up until then, we mostly only saw dad when he brought presents for me, and my twin brother Ron, at Christmas. That night, in the course of dinner conversation, my dad suddenly asked if I wanted to ride with him on the job. What? Are you kidding? Of course, I wanted to do that. This was better than any Christmas present!

In those days, the late 1930s, it was allowed. Dad told me the chief had no problem with it as long as my safety was a primary consideration.

We both knew, however, that we had to clear this with my mother, so we drove to her house and I asked her permission. She must have seen how excited I was, and she knew that dad would never put me in harm's way. She told me that as long as I was careful and didn't take any chances, it was all right with her.

As a detective, he had the freedom to work whatever shifts he needed to do his job. That meant that I spent days and evenings and sometimes even a late night working on every kind of case that was assigned to him. Being a detective doesn't give you the luxury to just work the "prime" cases. You work what the Detective Bureau sergeant assigns to you. Dad worked murders, gambling investigations, thefts, burglaries, rapes, suicides and on and on. Looking back, I realize I was exposed to a lot of things that must seem pretty outrageous to parents of today, things that most young people are steered away from; but, to me, being with him and watching him work was a vital part of the man I was to become.

I remember some of his cases as if they happened yesterday. I remember how dad worked on the theft of fishing gear from a sporting goods store, and how dogged he was with one particular suicide case. Dad was extremely detailed and very thorough, and he explained to me what he was doing and why he was doing it. He always talked to me as though I were a "rookie" in training. He taught me to cover all bases in any investigation. He stressed that you always start at the core of what you know, and work from there. "Don't set aside anything that catches your eye even if you think it's not important," he would say. If the thought occurred, there might be a good reason to look into it. He showed me time and time again how one small detail can lead you in the right direction to solve the case. While I didn't know it at the time, my instincts were being honed for police work from a very young age.

It wasn't always a bed of roses … we were both strong-willed, and the older I got, the more often we butted heads. One of the worst times we had was during my first year in college. I was playing football, which I loved, but studying accounting at my dad's insistence, which I hated. He said that if I wanted to get into the FBI, I had to have a law or accounting degree. He set his mind on the latter as the way I should go, but I got fed up with the course work and the direction my life was taking. I left school, went to the Army recruitment office, and joined up. When my dad found out, he was furious. He couldn't accept or understand my decision, and we didn't speak for the four years I was in the military, stationed in Japan and Korea.

Even after that estrangement, my father was the first person I went to see when I was discharged and came home. We spent the afternoon together, talking and healing the rift of the past years, then we went to see my mom, whom I hadn't seen for three years.

My dad was a tough cop, with a stubborn streak a mile wide, but he was also a gentleman when he needed to be. I saw the whole man, and picked the parts of him that I liked. Those qualities have stayed with me, and I'm a lot like him to this day.

Being around my father and his work, from that early age until I graduated from high school, gave me an advantage that many of my fellow FBI agents never had. I gained years of experience by riding with him. Those years gave me confidence when I entered the Bureau, and many of the assignments were "old hat" to me. That confidence also carried over into the attitude with which I approached my work: I wasn't there to please anyone but myself; just to do my job to the best of my ability.

On my first day as a new trainee in the FBI, I still hadn't decided whether I would go to see Deke, as he had instructed me to do. But after I walked into the classroom and met my fellow trainees, I decided not to go see him. I knew there might be repercussions – with Deke, with the FBI or with my dad – but I decided to just wait and see.

I was nearing the end of the 14 weeks, absorbed with the extensive training and feeling confident that Deke had forgotten about me.

I was in class one morning and feeling pleased at having received my first assignment, the Atlanta Office. Suddenly, one of the Bureau supervisors assigned to our class came over to me and said, "I don't know what you did, but Assistant Director DeLoach is madder than hell, and he wants you in his office right now." He told me to get a move on because "he's one guy you don't want to make any madder than he already is."

I immediately left the classroom and walked the several blocks to Deke's office, which was directly across the hall from the office of Director Hoover. I entered the reception area and identified myself to his secretary, who told me to take a seat. I could see Deke standing behind his desk, reading something.

He just stood there, making no effort to look up or out to the reception area. My mind was racing trying to determine what he was going to do. The morning passed, I continued to sit, and Deke continued to stand behind his desk reading. Sometime in the first hour of the afternoon he finally told his secretary to have me come in.

As a new agent, I was on probation for a year, and that made me vulnerable to anything Deke wanted to do. I knew he had power over me. I was just hoping he wouldn't fire me.

I walked in, shook his hand, and he told me to take a seat. Then he went back to reading from what I could now see was a stack of newspapers on his desk. He said nothing for the longest time, and I realized he was playing a psychological game to stress me out.

Out of the clear blue and without looking up at me, he finally asked, "Can you explain to me what you're trying to prove?"

He wanted an explanation as to why I had ignored his instructions about coming to his office on my first day of training, now many weeks ago. I told him that I had given it a lot of thought and decided I didn't want special treatment. I explained that I didn't want his close friendship with my dad to influence my career in the FBI.

"The street was made for my feet, and my feet were made for the street," I remember saying. Privately, I didn't want my dad to think any success I had was a result of his connections. Deke responded that since I had made that decision and followed through with it, I should return to my classes for the last few days in Washington. I knew there was no friendship between us but, with my career ahead of me, believed I could expect no interference from Deke DeLoach. As I look back on my 20 years of service with the FBI, I am grateful that this proved to be true. I also know with certainty that the self-confidence that stopped me from reporting to him on my first day in the Bureau was an essential part of the agent I became.

New FBI agent Don Adams – 1962

CHAPTER THREE

First Assignments: Atlanta and Thomasville

I was happy to learn that Atlanta was to be my first office of assignment. I am a small-town boy at heart and am not sure even now that I would have been happy in one of the bigger offices, such as New York, Chicago or Los Angeles.

I returned to Akron to spend the Christmas holidays at home, and then Jeanette, the kids and I left for Atlanta the day after New Year's, 1963. Knowing this first assignment was to be temporary, probably lasting one or two years, we settled into an apartment just northwest of the city.

Once in the Atlanta field office, I met Jim McMahon, the Special Agent in Charge of the office, who assigned me to the fugitive-bank robbery squad. My new supervisor was Ed Kassinger, and my first meeting with him was far from auspicious. During my service in Korea, I had contracted malaria and later had suffered two relapses. I'd had no further problems until, when I was standing at Kassinger's desk that day talking with him. I suddenly became very light-headed, broke into a cold sweat and proceeded to fall face-forward on top of his desk, breaking his pen set. An ambulance was called, and I was taken to the hospital where, once again, I was treated for malaria.

This incident was embarrassing, especially as I was just starting out in the office. Of course, my fellow agents kidded me about making a big impression by breaking the supervisor's pen set on the very first day, but Kassinger expressed deep concern for my well-being. I was lucky, as there were other supervisors who would have taken this incident in a very different way. Kassinger was a good guy who treated me fairly. He also knew the street and understood what had to be done to get good results.

I settled into the routine of the office. SAC McMahon and I had very little contact until several weeks later when he asked me to come to his office. He explained that I was to be transferred to the Thomasville, Georgia, Resident Agency. He said it was a one-man agency and that the senior resident agent there was Royal A. McGraw, for whom I would be working. The Thomasville Resident Agency was located 35 miles north of Tallahassee, Fla., near the state line. The Thomasville agency was responsible for nine counties, and the investigations of federal violations involved interstate trafficking from Georgia into Florida and Alabama and from Florida and Alabama into Georgia. The cases on which I was to be working would be predominantly automobile thefts and subsequent transportation of stolen vehicles across the state line, as well as fugitives fleeing to avoid confinement or prosecution.

In addition to filling me in on the basics of my new posting, McMahon told me it was unique for me to be sent to a resident agency so early in my career. He said I was selected for the assignment because I was older than the majority of new agents going into the field, an asset that would enable me to handle my assignments with less difficulty. He added that my past military service was another consideration.

I felt comfortable going to Thomasville. Having grown up around my dad during his years as a detective and accompanied him to various crime scenes gave me a sense of confidence that I could handle whatever task was presented to me.

One of the senior agents in the Atlanta office with whom I had become good friends was Brian O'Shea. "Osh," as he was called, looked out for me and gave me good, solid advice on cases. I met with him almost every morning before work over several cups of coffee, and we talked about many things but mostly about the Bureau.

From Osh I learned that three other agents in the office had earlier refused the assignment in Thomasville before McMahon dropped it on me. I was surprised that neither he nor the other agents I told about the transfer had mentioned that. In those days the FBI operated strictly on a "need-to-know basis." There was a clandestine "top secret" attitude prevalent within the Bureau that I disliked. If it involved privacy in an ongoing or pending investigation that was one thing, but too often I found this attitude extending to the way the Bureau dealt with its agents on broader matters. The information about the refusal of the other three agents to accept the transfer was not pertinent to any case, so I wondered about the secrecy. After I realized that I was his fourth choice, I felt like a fool. He had given the impression that he had singled me out because of my abilities, and I immediately lost a degree of trust in McMahon. I had come to appreciate, even during training, the straightforward and openly honest agent, whatever his status in the Bureau. Now I felt doubt about McMahon, and while I didn't know it at the time, that doubt would be fully justified in the years to come.

I started asking more questions. Answers were difficult to come by and guarded at best. Two of the three agents admitted they refused the job because of McGraw. Though the third agent would not tell me his reasons, he did say he would have quit the FBI rather than accept the transfer.

The next time I had a chance meeting with McMahon, I asked him outright if what I had learned was true. I could tell by the look on his face that he was very surprised and angered that someone had spilled the beans. He pressed me for the name of the source; I replied that I had learned it in general conversations.

McMahon admitted the information was true, but said all three agents had refused for personal reasons and it had nothing to do with McGraw. That was the second time he lied to me.

I was to start in Thomasville as a road-trip agent until my transfer came in. This meant I would maintain my office of assignment in Atlanta, along with our family's residence there, but I would work out of Thomasville, 240 miles away. For almost four months I packed a bag, left home on Sunday afternoon, and spent the week in Thomasville, returning the following Saturday.

During those four months, FBI Headquarters in Washington turned down the transfer twice, saying both times that I was too new in the field, before I was finally transferred there officially in June 1963.

The first time I went to Thomasville, I left Atlanta on a Sunday afternoon in the Bureau car assigned to me. As soon as I arrived, I went to a phone booth and called agent McGraw at his home to tell him I was in town. I asked him when we could meet to discuss my duties, and he said that he would see me Monday morning at 7 A.M.

I was about to ask a second time to meet with him before the next morning when he said, "I don't mean five minutes to seven or five minutes after seven, I mean seven o'clock."

The tone of his voice said it all and immediately made clear to me why those three agents didn't want to go to work in the Thomasville Resident Agency. After my first encounter with McGraw, all I could think was, "What the hell did I get myself into?"

The next morning, I found a restaurant and had an early breakfast. It was one of the town's main hangouts in the center of the three-block long downtown. The locals kept glancing at me, wondering who this stranger in the immaculate suit was.

After breakfast, I headed for the U.S. Post Office Building, which housed the FBI Office. I walked in and climbed the stairs to the hallway on the second floor. It was about ten minutes to seven. I sat on a table in the hallway and waited until I heard the sound of cleats on the marble steps leading up from the first floor.

It was exactly 7 A.M., and there stood Royal McGraw, a man of my height but a little heavier, with a square-jawed face that could have been carved out of granite. A former captain in the U.S. Marine Corps, he had retained the stature and proud bearing of that service. He walked over to me.

"Are you Don Adams?"

I told him I was.

"What time did you arrive at the office?"

I told him about 10 minutes ago.

He was visibly angry.

"I told you to be here at seven, not five minutes before or five minutes after."

He asked me if I could follow orders or was it necessary to send me back to Atlanta?

Inside, I was fuming, but before I could respond, he turned, unlocked and opened the door to the office, walked over to the only desk in the little room and sat down behind it.

The room had a sink, a filing cabinet and one chair behind a desk, nothing more. McGraw put his briefcase on the desk and very deliberately removed papers from it. He never looked up as he told me I was not to work off "his" desk. He said I would either do my paper work away from the office or, if necessary, I could use the top of the filing cabinet.

Royal McGraw and Don Adams, Atlanta, 1963.

I asked if it was okay to use his desk when he was out on the road. He said he had told me what I was to do, and that was it.

McGraw then told me to wait until the Post Office opened, go to the postal window, show my credentials and introduce myself. I was then to ask for the FBI mail and bring it to him.

"You are never to open any of the mail that comes to the office," he said, adding that this was his duty as the Senior Resident Agent.

He asked me if I understood his instructions, and I acknowledged I did. That was our first meeting, and everything went downhill from there for the next 18 months.

During the first weeks in Thomasville, McGraw had me drive him around so he could introduce me to the police chiefs and sheriffs in the nine counties we covered. One such introduction was to A.E. White, the sheriff of Bainbridge, Georgia.

When I met White he was wearing a white cowboy hat and leaning back in his chair with his cowboy boots propped on top of his desk. We exchanged pleasantries, and I asked to use the men's room.

"Why don't you use my 'john,'" he said pointing to a door in his office.

Through the door, I clearly heard McGraw tell the sheriff to be careful dealing with me because "he's a Catholic, a Republican and a Yankee."

That taught me that as a "good old Georgia boy," McGraw had more allegiance to the South than to a fellow agent, especially if that agent happened to be a "Catholic, a Republican and a Yankee."

The daily routine varied little; however, McGraw circumvented normal FBI procedure. Each morning, he would open and review the mail, then hand me the cases he decided I should work. He would often give me cases with his name in the block stamp, meaning they had been assigned to him, at the same time taking cases with my name in the block stamp for himself. McGraw would simply call the field office and have the cases reassigned, which was contrary to standard operating procedure. The supervisors in Atlanta apparently overlooked the irregularity and made the changes he requested.

Whenever I tried to question McGraw about anything beyond mundane matters, he instantly shut me down. My upbringing and military service had indoctrinated me with respect for authority, so I complied. I followed his orders and dropped any questions he chose not to answer. Being stubborn, I was determined to finish out my Thomasville assignment no matter what.

Little did I know at the time, McGraw was setting a precedent for actions that would affect the course of history.

CHAPTER FOUR

Two Plots to Kill

Working with McGraw never got any easier. More often than not, I would take the cases handed to me, leave the office and work elsewhere. After I completed a good day's work, I would head to a restaurant in whatever county I was working and rough-draft reports from my investigative notes. I don't think McGraw ever did figure out how I was able to keep up with my paper work.

When a new federal building was completed some months later, the Thomasville Resident Agency moved in and there were desks for both of us, so I could finally work in the office.

With all the difficulty I had in developing a working relationship with McGraw, he was a master at report writing, and he taught me well. This was self-serving to a great degree, and had more to do with his performance rating than any desire to be a mentor. As the Senior Resident Agent, he was responsible for my level of competence. If I did a good job, his performance rating reflected that, which in turn affected the ratings of his immediate superiors and so on up the chain of command. Nonetheless, after a few months with McGraw, I never had a report returned for rewriting. It's a shame he wasn't as talented when it came to dealing with people.

I worked a lot of different cases in Thomasville. There were many fugitives caught, we solved a number of stolen car and other federal cases, and worked a Cuban lottery case for months, during which McGraw and I conducted surveillances for long hours together in one car.

After just 10 months in the field, I received a phone call that would change my life.

It was dinnertime on Wednesday, Nov. 13, 1963, when Atlanta SAC McMahon called me at home. He told me that a matter of the utmost urgency had just been brought to his attention, and he wanted me to begin an investigation the first thing in the morning. McMahon said he had received a call from the agent in charge of the Secret Service in Atlanta asking for FBI assistance, since the Secret Service had no agents in South Georgia. The matter was "top priority," he said, adding that I should devote as much time as necessary until my investigation was completed.

McMahon told me that a reliable informant with both the Miami Police Department and the Miami FBI office had furnished information about an October 1963 meeting of a radical, right-wing hate group in a hotel in Indianapolis, Indiana. According to the informant, he and three other men had privately discussed a plot to kill President John F. Kennedy. The informant said that one of the four men in the discussion was a sniper in World War II and was willing to sacrifice his life to kill the President.

Kennedy regularly flew into Homestead Air Force Base in Florida and then traveled in the presidential limousine, usually with the top down, along Collins Avenue to the Kennedy compound in Palm Beach. The plan was to have the sniper secrete himself in one of the palm trees along Collins Avenue and shoot the President as his car passed by.

Though they believed this Florida scenario would work, a back-up plan was also discussed. This involved renting an apartment or office located behind Lafayette Park in Washington, D.C., directly across from the White House. The informant said they talked about setting up a large-caliber, scoped rifle on a tripod and shooting the President as he walked around the White House grounds.

McMahon then related to me that the informant had contacted the Miami Police Department, who notified the Secret Service.

According to McMahon, the principal subject was a Joseph Adams Milteer of Quitman, Georgia. McMahon said he wanted me to conduct an extensive background investigation on Milteer as quickly as possible. When the investigation was completed, McMahon said, all of the information should be turned over to him to be disseminated to the Secret Service. He then cautioned me not to discuss this matter with anyone.

I said that would impose unacceptable difficulties, since this type of investigation would require the help of others. McMahon was adamant, repeating that he wanted me to do this alone and talk with no one about it. Again, I stressed that with all of the contacts that had to be made, as quickly as possible, I could not do this investigation alone. I mentioned Bill Elliott, the Quitman chief of police, as the one person I knew I could count on to help me get the information discreetly.

McMahon questioned me about Elliott, and I explained that I had worked with him on several matters in the past months and considered him trustworthy. He finally agreed to involve Elliott, as long as he understood the confidentiality of the matter and the need for haste.

I called and arranged to meet Elliott that evening in Quitman. After I explained the situation, the chief agreed to help, consenting to discuss our work with no one. It may sound overdramatic, but I remember being impressed when Elliott said he would give his life, if required, to complete this investigation.

We began the next day. Quitman was a small town where everybody knew each other, and Elliott was aware of Milteer. We checked his residence; he was not there, nor was his VW bus to be found anywhere in town. We learned through inquiry that Milteer had been dating and at times living with a woman

One of Milteer's many Volkswagens.

C.C. Cofield & J.A. Milteer

named C.C. Cofield in Valdosta, Georgia, so we traveled there to confer with the police chief. After obtaining information from him about Milteer and Cofield, we continued inquiries with other agencies, checked Cofield's residence and gathered some solid background information.

Joseph Adams Milteer was born in February 26, 1902 in Quitman, Georgia, where he lived alone in a large-run-down house. He had gray, partial thinning hair, wore glasses, was often unshaven and generally dressed in old clothes. He had no family, no friends, no relatives nearby, and no employment. In 1955, he had been arrested for suspicion of burglary in Valdosta, and had been released.

A wealthy bachelor, Milteer had inherited an estimated $200,000 from his father, and never bought anything on credit. He was a prolific pamphlet writer and spent a great deal of time travelling throughout the Southeast advocating for various

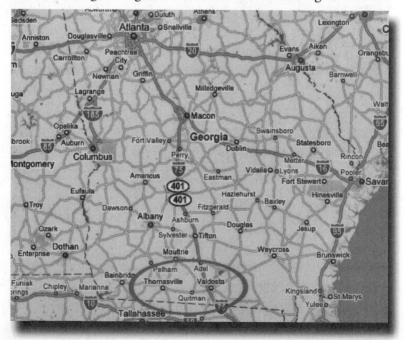

radical political parties. He had run unsuccessfully for local office and published a weekly tract criticizing local government.

Our investigation continued the following day, Friday, both in Quitman and Valdosta, but we were unsuccessful in locating either Milteer or a photo of him. After hours of searching the fingerprint files at the Lowndes County Jail, we finally found a card for Milteer in a basement file cabinet. It was after midnight, but I was elated. The sergeant at the desk of the Lowndes County Sheriff's office in Valdosta told us that the fingerprint card on Milteer was the only one on file. He asked that the card be returned to their office when we were finished with it. I assured him that I would tell my superiors about his request and would also mention it in my report.

This was 2 A.M. when we returned to the Cofield residence and through surveillance located the vehicles of both Milteer and Cofield, making note of license plates with detailed descriptions.

It was Saturday, Nov. 16, three days since McMahon's call. Elliott had told me that Milteer passed out hate literature every Saturday in downtown Quitman, and this Saturday should be no different. I wanted to see this suspect up close, so I dressed in old work clothes to allay any suspicion, and Elliott and I went to find Milteer.

I separated from Bill a couple of blocks from where Milteer was standing, then walked down and loitered behind him for a while. I then moved next to him, engaging him in general conversation. Within minutes, he started talking about how much he hated the Kennedys and what needed to be done to them, but he was very careful not to make a direct threat. He gave me a number of different copies of the material he was passing out. His propaganda clearly confirmed that he was a radical segregationist. He hated blacks, Yankees and many others.

Bill and I attempted to take a surveillance photograph of him but were unable to get in a proper position to do so.

Having gathered the information I had been asked to compile, I returned to Thomasville and prepared a rough-draft report. This included enclosures of all of the materials we had obtained from all of the agencies and sources, as well as the large stack of mimeographed hate brochures I had received from Milteer. I was as thorough as possible because of the importance of the situation, and I was confident that my investigation was complete. I drove all the way to Atlanta and hand-carried the documents to the office to be turned over to McMahon. I assumed that the information would be immediately routed to both FBI headquarters and the Secret Service; this was, after all, a report concerning a suspect who might be planning to assassinate the President. I also knew: procedure dictated that the original documents would remain with the FBI in Atlanta and copies would be furnished to the Secret Service.

It is only from the vantage point of hindsight that I have come to realize there were a number of inconsistencies and outright deceptions during my initial investigation of Milteer. I am convinced that I was being used as the "new kid on the block."

Why did I, a rookie agent, get the call from McMahon on Nov. 13? Why was such a critical investigation not given to my supervisor Royal McGraw, a far more experienced agent? Why did McGraw never question my whereabouts during the days I investigated Milteer? McMahon must have told him what I was doing; yet he never acknowledged it, contrary to his previous iron-handed control, often taking my assigned cases and/or giving me his. Why would he pass on a matter of such national importance? It is possible McMahon didn't want McGraw to know what I was doing, but subsequent events don't support such a theory.

In addition, I now know that the Atlanta FBI Office had conducted a previous investigation of Milteer in the autumn of 1962 under the title, "Racial Matters," conducted by Agent Royal A. McGraw, with the assistance of Quitman Chief of Police Bill Elliott. This was just one year before I was assigned to investigate Milteer. Strangely, I was not informed of that. I spent many hours with Chief Elliott during the 1963 investigation and at no time did he ever mention having worked the subject before. McGraw should have told me as a matter of routine FBI procedure. And that as we will see, was not all that was kept from me.

The only conclusion I can come to is that there was collusion between McMahon, McGraw and Elliott to withhold substantive information from me about Milteer. The reasons for this I cannot determine with absolute certainty, but that does not change the facts – facts that smack of that dreaded word, *conspiracy*. Forty-four years later, when I was at the National Archives to review the files pertaining to Milteer and the Kennedy assassination, I found a copy of a communication sent by the FBI in Atlanta to the FBI Identification Division in Washington, D.C. That communication requested that the fingerprints of Milteer should be returned to the provider. A follow-up communication indicated the fingerprints were in fact returned to the Valdosta Police Department, so that confirmed to me that the fingerprint card I had found did go through the appropriate channels. Yet, *nothing else of my initial report could be found*, including the stack of hate propaganda given me by Milteer. It was gone.

The two specific assassination plots discussed that October day in Indianapolis were not carried out. Whether it was due to the informant's tip or not, the Secret Service put in place precautions during President Kennedy's speech in Miami on Monday, Nov. 18. Instead of traveling by motorcade from Homestead Air Force Base, he was transported to the speech site by helicopter.

Four days later, Friday, Nov. 22, 1963 the president would be in Dallas.

Dealey Plaza
Dallas, Texas

CHAPTER FIVE

Assassination's Wake

Like most of the American public that weekend in November 1963, my wife Jeanette and I were glued to the television. But I also had my important new assignment given to me on the afternoon of the assassination by Atlanta's SAC MacMahon to locate and interview Joseph Milteer. So, for the next five days, three times a day, I drove the twenty miles to Quitman and another twenty miles to Valdosta (and back again) looking for Milteer. In between all this traveling something very strange happened.

On Sunday morning, Nov. 24, the front doorbell rang, and Jeanette went to answer it. I heard some conversation, and then I heard Jeanette scream. I ran to the door and saw a women standing there with her hand in her purse. I grabbed her and put her up against the wall, thinking she was reaching for a weapon. The lady said she was just getting her driver's license and identified herself as Vereen Alexander. Jeanette explained that the woman had asked if this was the home of FBI Agent Don Adams, and then reached into her purse. Not knowing who she was, Jeanette had panicked.

Once we all relaxed, Ms. Alexander told me she had come to find me because she knew Lee Harvey Oswald, and wanted to explain her involvement with him. It turned out that she was the daughter of a Federal judge and a student at Tulane University in New Orleans. She recounted the story of an evening earlier in the year, when she and a group of students were seated around a table at a local bar. The topic of discussion, she said, was the attempted assassination six months earlier of President Charles de Gaulle of France. She remembered a question being asked about how one would assassinate the President of the United States. The person who asked that question, according to Alexander, was Lee Harvey Oswald.

I obtained the details about this discussion, including the names of the people at the table, and she left.

I immediately prepared a report for the Atlanta office and had them send the information to Washington D.C., Dallas and New Orleans, with a request for an investigation at Tulane University to verify the identities of all persons involved in her story.

I continued checking for Milteer three times each day, as did Chief Elliott and the Valdosta sheriff, but he was nowhere to be found.

Then, late in the afternoon of Wednesday, Nov. 27 – five days after the assassination – I observed a VW bus at Cofield's address. Agency procedure required that I have back-up before confronting Milteer, so I went to a pay phone and called in FBI agent Ken Williams, the Valdosta Resident Agent.

We met at a pre-arranged location, I briefed him, and we both drove back to the Cofield address. The VW bus was gone. We confronted Cofield, and she said Milteer was headed north toward Atlanta, and that she didn't expect him back for some time.

Ken and I hopped in our separate cars and drove north some 54 miles before we spotted the VW bus. I pulled in front of Milteer, forcing him to come to a stop, jumped from my car and quickly had him out and on the side of his vehicle. I checked him for a weapon and found none.

We called for a Georgia Highway Patrolman and a tow truck to take the VW bus back to the Valdosta Highway Patrol Post. Before the tow truck arrived, Milteer told me he hadn't eaten and asked if he could take his dinner with him, which he indicated to be in a paper bag. I looked at the top of the bag and saw a banana, so I told him OK. Milteer got into the seat next to me for the ride back to the Resident Agency in Valdosta. Agent Williams followed us in his car.

Once back at the Valdosta FBI office, Milteer set the bag on the desk while I proceeded to interview him. First, I obtained detailed descriptive data and then started to ask him the five questions that McMahon had allowed me. At this point, Milteer interrupted.

"I know that you're tape recording my conversation," he said. I told him he was not being taped, but his statement bothered me. I walked around the desk to the paper bag, removed the banana and a napkin, and found a tape recorder with the reels spinning. *He was taping our conversation!*

I shut the machine off and removed the tape, thinking he had some nerve to tape an interview with the FBI. I was struck by how brazen Milteer was, and how my carelessness in not checking the bag, especially for a weapon, could have had deadly consequences.

I then proceeded with the five questions I had been limited to by SAC McMahon:

1) With whom had he made contact recently?

He said he went to Dallas, Texas in June of 1963 in an attempt to persuade Dan Smoot, author of "The Dan Smoot Report," to run as a candidate for Vice President on the Constitution Party ticket in November 1964. He said he had no other business in Dallas during his visit there.

2) Had he been to the Constitution Party's National Convention?

He answered yes, and said the convention was held in Indianapolis, Indiana, Oct. 18-20, 1963. He went as a guest of Curtis B. Dall, former son-in-law of the late President Franklin D. Roosevelt. He traveled with two friends, Bill Somersett of Miami, Florida, and Lee McCloud of Atlanta.

3) What were the organizations with which he was affiliated?

He answered that he considered himself a non-dues-paying member of the White Citizen's Council of Atlanta, Georgia; that he was a member of the Congress of Freedom, and the Constitution Party. He said that during April 1963, he attended a national convention in New Orleans of the Congress of

Freedom. I was itching to ask him if he was a member of the Ku Klux Klan, as I had been told, but the orders from McMahon precluded that question.

4) Had he any knowledge of the bombing of the 16th Street Baptist Church in Birmingham, Alabama, on Sept. 15, 1963?
He denied having any knowledge of that bombing.

5) Had he ever made any threats to assassinate the President, or had he participated in a plot to kill President Kennedy?
He emphatically denied ever doing such a thing and said he never heard anyone else make such threats. He said that he never made any threats against anyone before the assassination took place. He said he didn't know, nor, to his knowledge, was he ever in the presence of Lee Harvey Oswald or "Jack Ruby."

I interviewed Milteer until the early morning hours of Thursday, Nov. 28, 1963, getting as much information as possible within the narrow parameters allowed me. Since he was not under arrest, photographs and fingerprints were not taken.

When we finished, he left the office and went on his way. It was the last time I ever saw Milteer ... in person.

I prepared the written, rough-draft report and a teletype for FBI HQ. Then I dictated them both, by telephone, to a steno at the Atlanta FBI Office late that same morning, ensuring that the Special Agent in Charge would receive the report as quickly as possible.

I cannot to this day confirm that my second report on Milteer ever reached the appropriate persons or went through the proper channels. Like my first report on Milteer, these documents have seemingly disappeared; there are no copies to be found in any of the files I have searched at the National Archives.

Some of the information I gathered eventually surfaced in subsequent reports related to the assassination, filed in December 1963 by FBI Special Agents Charles Harding and Ken Williams, and in January 1964 by Royal McGraw. It appears they cherry-picked what they wanted from my investigative results and incorporated that information into their own reports. The documentation that show this, as well as other fraudulent aspects of those reports, only came to light during my follow-up research years later. When I filed my last report on Milteer in 1963, I had no reason to doubt that my investigations were complete and accurate, or that proper procedures had been observed. Nearly a year after I filed those reports, the Warren Commission officially confirmed Lee Harvey Oswald as the lone assassin of President John F. Kennedy. Joseph Adams Milteer was no longer of interest to me … until some 30 years later.

CHAPTER SIX

Transfer to Texas

In June of 1964, I was transferred to the FBI Office in Dallas.

The Special Agent in Charge of the Dallas office was J. Gordon Shanklin, and in our first meeting, he told me that the Kennedy assassination was still Priority No. One. Shanklin said I would be covering leads as they developed. To better prepare for this assignment, he told me to spend my first few days in the office watching the Abraham Zapruder film and visiting the Texas School Book Depository.

I observed that my new SAC's ashtray was always overflowing with cigarette butts, and he would often light his next cigarette from the one he was still smoking. His nails and fingers were stained brown. He reminded me of a railroad steam engine, puffing smoke as it chugged down the track. Some of the agents called him "snowflake" because his coat was often covered with ashes, not to mention little burn holes at various locations in his ties, shirts, suit jackets and trousers.

As I saw it, Shanklin's major weakness was his fear of doing anything that could create problems for him with the top administration in Washington. The basic

J. Gordon Shanklin

Hoover decree was, "Don't embarrass the Bureau," or shed a bad light on "his" FBI. I became convinced that Shanklin would do anything to avoid this. That conviction grew during several occasions over the years when he and I worked together closely on investigations. The man was scared of his own shadow.

As requested, I spent my first days in Dallas familiarizing myself with the evidence. There were two large rooms within the Dallas FBI Office; one was named the John Kennedy room and the second was the Oswald room. A massive amount of paper had been generated in the seven months since Nov. 22, 1963. The Kennedy room had five-drawer filing cabinets stuffed into every space available on all four walls. Each cabinet was stuffed to capacity with documents. The Oswald room was much the same, but contained fewer cabinets.

It was in the Kennedy room that I watched the Zapruder film with two senior Dallas agents. As the three of us watched the film on a large screen, sitting approximately eight to 10 feet back, details emerged that can't be seen in photographs or on a regular TV screen.

As soon as the president's limousine came out from behind the sign and I saw him raise his elbows into the air and his hands go to his throat, I blurted out, "Hell that shot didn't come from the rear: it came from the front."

Then came the head shot. I observed how his head was flung backwards, with a large piece of skull and brain matter exploding into a mist to the left rear of the car.

One of the two agents cautioned me to say nothing, adding that it had already been determined that Oswald shot the President from the rear out of a sixth-floor window at the Book Depository.

I remember saying at the time, "That's bullshit."

I am a Korean War veteran who saw serious action, and I know where a shot would have to come from for President Kennedy to react as he did. The three of us discussed this, but both agents stood firm, and warned me again that what I was implying could cause me problems. Still, I had seen what I had seen, and that led to only one conclusion: the president had been shot from the front!

A couple of days later I went to the Texas School Book Depository, accompanied by two other senior agents. We went to the sixth-floor window from which Oswald was alleged to have shot the President.

I went around the barricade in front of the window, to get a better look down onto Houston and Elm streets. The window was open – it was a hot day in June – and I looked down on the route Kennedy's car traveled. Directly in my line of sight was a tree in full foliage. I asked about the tree's foliage back in November. They assured me it would have been the same, because the summer lasts longer down south and the tree would have been in full foliage now as it was in November.

View from the 6th floor.

"What was the time sequence and number of shots fired by Oswald?" I asked.

One of the agents said Oswald fired three shots in 7.5 seconds with a bolt-action, scoped rifle and that all three were on target. I looked out the window again, and noticed that the tree had an opening at the top, separating the leaves. Again, I asked if Oswald had fired the shots with the tree in the same condition. The agent replied that the tree had not changed too much from the day of the shooting.

"There is no way Oswald fired three shots in a little over 7 seconds with a scoped, bolt-action rifle and made the hits he supposedly made," I said, again relying on my war-time experience.

Eerily, like déjà vu, both agents cautioned me to keep any unorthodox observations to myself; essentially the same thing the other two agents had told me a few days earlier.

I only spent a few months in Dallas before being transferred to Lubbock, Texas, but I made it a point to have general discussions about the Kennedy shooting with some of the Dallas agents. To a man, they were all very cautious about discussing the worst crime we had ever known. Less than a year after the assassination, on Sept. 27, 1964, the Warren Commission made public its 888-page final report. After the testimony of more than 500 witnesses and the viewing of some 3,000 exhibits, the report named Lee Harvey Oswald as the sole shooter responsible for the assassination of President Kennedy and the wounding of Texas Gov. John Connally.

I knew in my gut this finding was at least premature. After viewing the Zapruder film and visiting the Texas School Book Depository, I could not reconcile the Warren Commission's findings with what I had observed, both from my background as a Korean War veteran and a trained law enforcement agent.

But I still had less than two years of field experience under my belt, and a wife and family to support. I had already been cautioned several times by more experienced agents that the case was virtually closed, and that I needed to keep quiet about any observations and conclusions to the contrary. I knew they had acted in good faith to protect me from what they saw as a threat to my career so, despite my misgivings, I walked away and kept my head down.

What could I possibly add, I asked myself, to a fully empowered government commission whose members were high-ranking and well-respected men with total access to all investigative information compiled by the best law enforcement agency in the world ... the FBI? In other words, like most Americans in 1964, I trusted my government.

The Warren Report's findings ended the chapter of my life concerning the assassination of our 35th President ... or so I thought.

The Warren Commission

I was in Lubbock for three years, until September 1967, when I was transferred back to the Dallas FBI office for one year. Along the way, I worked many cases: finding and arresting military deserters, in one case a lieutenant colonel; busting (on federal and local charges) a burglary ring at Dallas Love Airport following a four month-long investigation; building a case to put a habitual criminal in prison for life. I loved my job, plugged away, and dug deeply into each case, often working with local authorities with whom I developed good relationships.

This was not always the case between the Dallas FBI office and the Dallas Police Department.

I learned of two incidents in particular that soured what should have been symbiotic relationships among FBI agents and Dallas police officers. Following the Kennedy assassination, Agent Vince Drain arbitrarily took what became known as the Oswald rifle out of the Dallas Police Department's control and flew it to FBI Headquarters in Washington. Needless to say, this did not sit well with the local authorities.

Then there was the matter of a local police detective who spent months compiling a book identifying all of the thieves living in north Texas and especially the Dallas area. Somehow, the book ended up in the hands of a Dallas FBI agent, who was brazen enough to copy the entire book and then turn it in to the chief of police, taking credit for all the work. Once this deception became known in the Dallas Police Department, the FBI became a collective persona non grata.

James Hosty

CHAPTER SEVEN

Fidelity, Bravery, Integrity?

After my assignments to Dallas, Lubbock and then back to Dallas, I was transferred to the Buffalo FBI office. My principal duty was as bank robbery coordinator for the Buffalo Field Division. I also assisted in organized-crime investigations, especially in the arrests and detention of subjects. In addition, I helped fellow agents in the arrests of other subjects for federal law violations, and finally worked at Attica Penitentiary, in Attica N.Y., to assist with and clean up a number of federal violations that occurred inside the prison. After four years in Buffalo I was sent to northeast Ohio and returned to live in my hometown of Akron. In 1975, I was in my Bureau car when I heard a radio broadcast that caught my attention. It was a news report about the destruction of a threatening letter, written by Lee Harvey Oswald, which had been delivered to the Dallas FBI office a week or two before the Kennedy assassination.

According to the news story, FBI Dallas office clerk Nan Fenner knew about the letter and its contents. She reportedly stated that in the letter, Oswald threatened to either shoot FBI Agent James Hosty or blow up the Dallas FBI office. Both of those allegations were serious enough that, per normal Bureau procedure, they should have been written up at that time. Had that been done, the information noting Oswald as a person to watch – regardless of whether he had made a threat against the president – would have been provided to the Secret Service before and during the president's visit that November.

Why would a serious threat of this kind be ignored and not passed on to the agency charged with safeguarding the life of the president? If Oswald was the assassin, and had this letter been turned over to the advance Secret Service team, would JFK have left Dallas alive? We will never know.

I have come to believe that the Secret Service was not informed of Oswald's "threat," according to standard Bureau protocol, for one primary reason – Oswald must have been a government informant for the CIA, the FBI or both. That is the only reasonable explanation I can find for the lack of notification, as well as for his movements, before, during and even after the assassination.

There was one other interesting facet of that newscast; I learned that it was J. Gordon Shanklin, the Special Agent in Charge in Dallas and my former superior, who had ordered Hosty to destroy Oswald's letter. That corroborated my experience with Shanklin, and confirmed that it was not the only time Shanklin was responsible for the destruction of documents.

During my years in the Lubbock office, I too was the victim of Shanklin's propensity to destroy documents that could shed a less than positive light on his performance. In my case, it involved an incident that Shanklin did not want FBI officials in the Washington headquarters to learn about.

I had been assigned the boss's year-old car. It's standard procedure that he is given a new car every year. Shanklin had tagged the older car for my use only, but before I could take possession, another agent took it out, against Bureau policy, only to be involved in an accident with extensive damage to the car. Since the agent had to pay for the repairs out of his own pocket, he took the car to the shop of one of the office's informants. I questioned the completeness of the repairs, but he assured me several times that the work was handled competently.

I received a telephone call from the Dallas office telling me the car was repaired and ready for me to pick up. I flew into Dallas the next morning, got the keys and left for Lubbock immediately. Just a short while after I got onto the highway the hood popped up. I pulled over, and after slamming it down continued on my way. I didn't want to have any problems and I drove a slower speed so in case something happened I could stop the car safely. I didn't travel many more miles before the hood popped up again. I called Senior Resident Agent Aubrey Elliott in Lubbock and told him what was happening. I told him that I would take the car to the Ford garage as soon as I arrived and have them check the problem. The hood continued popping up. I estimate that it must have popped up about 17 times during the 360 mile trip.

I went to the garage and asked to have the car checked. The service manager said that the locking mechanism was not adjusted properly. He got his tool and made an adjustment on the latch. He slammed down the hood and attempted to lift it. He did this three times and it did not lift once. He said that should take care of it. I drove to our parking garage, locked the car and went to the office. I told Aubrey what had been done and he was satisfied.

The next morning I had work at Muleshoe, Texas which is located up in the corner of the Panhandle, near Clovis, New Mexico. I worked in the Sheriff's Office and covered some other leads in town. I had lunch and was working on cases that afternoon when the radio blurted out a message to call the FBI Office in Lubbock. I went to a pay phone and called. Aubrey told me that the two military deserters that were assigned to me had just gone to the Post Office. He said they told the postal employee they were going to their apartment. The case was assigned to me so I went to apprehend the subjects.

I was traveling south towards Lubbock when an approaching tractor trailer passed. The hood of the car flew up and flipped back down on my head, level with the top of the seats. I was knocked down to the passenger-side floorboards and the next thing I remember is being helped out of the car by a Good Samaritan, who had witnessed the accident. We somehow got the car back on the road, located the hood on the other side of the highway and I continued on my way, shaken up and in pain from the trauma to my head and neck. Nonetheless, I had a job to do.

This entire affair – the agent's misconduct; the bogus repairs leading to the accident; the resulting life-threatening injuries and back surgery; my Workman's Compensation claims, and the emotional and financial distress my family went through for more than two years – all of it was kept from Bureau officials by none other than the man whose name I had just heard on the radio – J. Gordon Shanklin.

In attempting to cover up his misdeeds, Shanklin nearly cost me my life and totally compromised my family's economic stability. He lied to me for more than two years about Worker's Compensation claims, while destroying my medical documents to cover his rear end. Nearly 10 years later, I was still trying to recover lost compensation as a result of Shanklin's misdeeds. Now, with the news report I had just heard, I had corroborating information that Shanklin had no problem destroying documents in violation of FBI rules and regulations.

At this point in my FBI career, I was not eligible to retire for another seven years. Even so, I decided to file a Freedom of Information Act request for FBI files concerning the destruction of documents by SAC Shanklin. At the time, I was more interested in how this information would affect my situation than whether it would shed light on anything else; however, given my current interest in the JFK assassination, it was sadly ironic. Prior to making my FOIA request, I spoke with close friends in the FBI, and they expressed concerns that Bureau personnel would do something to me for my actions. Nonetheless, after much thought, I filed the request.

When Bureau headquarters received my FOIA request, I got a phone call from an assistant director.

"Is there a certain document that you are looking for?" I remember his asking.

"My request is specific," I replied. "It asks for any information in Bureau files, dating back to 1960 and up to the date of my request, regarding any destruction of records by SAC Shanklin."

I had made the request all-inclusive, thinking that Shanklin may have destroyed other documents, given how fearful he was about causing problems for the Bureau. Any other documents found to have been destroyed would provide additional corroboration and buttress my case. I knew that most Bureau employees doing what Shanklin had done would have, at best, been terminated. At worst, that employee could have been prosecuted for the destruction of documents in a murder investigation, i.e. the Oswald letter and its tie-in to the Kennedy assassination.

A few days went by and I received another call, this time from a different assistant director asking the same question. I gave him the same response.

Another couple of days went by and for the third time, I received a call. This call was from an assistant director who later became Director of the FBI. He went "fishing" with me, but I stood my ground. Finally, he asked me directly – and he sounded angry – if I was asking for information concerning the destruction of a letter from Lee Harvey Oswald to Agent Jim Hosty, which had been received by the Dallas FBI office a week or two before President Kennedy was assassinated.

"Bingo, you hit it on the head," was my less than proper response from a street agent to an authority.

I could tell by the way he hung up that he was mad as hell.

Several days passed before I received a call from the SAC in Cleveland telling me an envelope had arrived from Bureau headquarters and was being held for me by Agent Scott Brantley, the office's legal agent. I drove to Cleveland that same day, itching to know what the envelope contained. Brantley handed it over, telling me the information was for my eyes only. I don't think Brantley ever knew what was in the envelope, given the Bureau's secretive modus operandi.

Anxious as I was to see the contents, I waited until I left Cleveland to pull off the road and open the envelope. There was nothing addressed to me – the Bureau obviously did not want any connection to my receipt of the documents – but there was a 27-page memo from Clarence Kelley, Director of the FBI, to Attorney General Edward Levi dated Oct. 1, 1975 and titled "Assassination of President John F. Kennedy." I was elated by what I read. Though he denied any knowledge of an Oswald note, Shanklin was implicated by numerous other sworn statements in the memo. To me, it was proof positive that Shanklin gave a direct order to Hosty to destroy the Oswald note. Shanklin's deception and destruction of documents would buttress my financial and medical case with the Bureau.

Far more alarming when viewed in light of the JFK assassination was the existence and then destruction of this threatening note. It had obviously been concealed from the Warren Commission by Shanklin and Hosty in Dallas, and most probably their superiors in Washington D.C., including Director Hoover. It led me to wonder if there was other information about the assassination that FBI officials had concealed, but I never thought to follow up at that time. Remember, the Warren Commission had been definitive in naming Oswald as the lone assassin, and whatever doubts I may have had flew in the face of recognized authority.

The Oswald note and its destruction was the last thing I remember being involved with concerning the assassination of President Kennedy until more than 15 years later, in December of 1992, 10 years after I retired from the FBI.

During the Christmas holidays of 1992, my wife and I were visiting with friends whose son, Larry Dannemiller, was home for the holidays from Houston, Texas. Larry knew I had been an FBI agent during the time of the JFK assassination and asked me if I was involved. I related the story of the threats made by Milteer shortly before JFK was killed, referring to him only as "Joseph A." Larry had been a very avid follower of the assassination controversy and he recommended a book that contained new information. About two months later, I received from Larry a copy of *High Treason*, co-authored by Robert Groden and Harrison Livingstone. When I opened the cover, I saw a note from Larry that read, "Joseph A. is mentioned in the back section. Good reading."

My assumption at that point was that Larry couldn't possibly be referring to Milteer. I had never used his last name. I thought it must be another Joseph A. involved in the assassination.

Joseph A is Mentioned in the Back Section Good reading - Larry

I turned to the index in the back of the book and was shocked to read "Joseph Milteer 11(n) and 358." That was the first time I had seen, heard or read the name Joseph Milteer since 1963, except in discussions with other agents.

I turned to page 11 and read that the Miami Police Department had a taped interview with police informant William Somersett in which Milteer discussed a plot to kill President Kennedy with a high-powered rifle from an office building. That sentence hit me like a bomb. As I continued reading, the other information I discovered in *High Treason* was even more devastating.

Milteer's involvement was recounted in an appendix, and after reading those two-and-a-half pages, I was dumbfounded. The Miami police and the FBI knew of this tape-recording before I was assigned to locate and interview Milteer, yet I had been told nothing about it! Something was drastically wrong. The Bureau that I had been part of and respected just did not work this way.

I started at the front of the book and leafed through the photographs, a number of which I had never seen before. About halfway through, I saw a face I immediately recognized. It was a photo of the man I knew as Joseph A. Milteer. Also on that page was a photo of William Somersett, the Miami Police Department's informant. Then I was drawn to the picture at the center of the page. There was Milteer, standing with a group of people in Dealey Plaza, looking toward the Presidential limousine: a photograph that had to have been taken just seconds before the President was shot.

I had been sure Milteer was not in Georgia on Nov. 22, 1963, and often wondered where he was. When I saw that photograph in *High Treason*, I finally knew. I can't put into words how I felt at that moment, but I became convinced, and still am, that President John Fitzgerald Kennedy should have survived that day in Dallas on Nov. 22, 1963.

High Treason changed my life, and started me on the search to uncover other inconsistencies in the investigation of the assassination of President Kennedy.

HIGH TREASON

THE ASSASSINATION OF PRESIDENT JOHN F. KENNEDY

WHAT REALLY HAPPENED

Robert J. Groden
Harrison Edward Livingstone

With an Article by Col. Fletcher Prouty

CHAPTER EIGHT

A Quest For the Truth

In 1993 I was still working in law enforcement, now Chief of Police for the city of Fairlawn, a small community just west of Akron. My interest and personal involvement in the JFK mystery was becoming known throughout area communities.

As the 30th anniversary drew near, a reporter from the *Akron Beacon Journal* asked me to write down some observations about the assassination. I complied and sent the reporter a summary version of my thoughts. A few days later, another *Beacon Journal* reporter called and asked for an interview. The interest from that article resulted in my being asked to speak about the assassination, and that in turn led to an expanding circle of information and contacts. People would frequently get in touch with me and provide documents or suggest reading to bolster my contentions. And though I spoke from personal experience, I also researched and learned as much as I could about what had happened that day in Dallas.

What I found confirmed my suspicions that the crime had been preventable. I built an ever-strengthening case for challenging the conclusions of the Warren Commission and reopening the investigation. After all the years of deception and destruction of documents, I was trying to get to the bottom of this murder once and for all.

After reading *High Treason*, I began to earnestly question the official verdict. I have come to understand many people did tell the truth, but that truth has been hidden from the public, sealed in the National Archives. Conversely, many people told lies to conceal that truth, and those lies derailed what was arguably the most important investigation the FBI has ever undertaken.

Among the lies I have confirmed is one of which I have personal knowledge and experience: the whereabouts of Joseph A. Milteer on the day of the assassination. I was sure that Milteer was not in Valdosta, nor was he in Quitman, Georgia, until five days after the assassination. And after discovering a photograph of him in *High Treason*, standing in Dealey Plaza moments before the assassination, I began looking for ways to corroborate just where he was. What I found in that search turned out to be even more disturbing.

FBI Teletype – November 22, 1963

I have copies of an FBI Teletype [**Doc. #1**], sent to the Director by Atlanta SAC McMahon in which it is falsely reported that Milteer was in Quitman at the time of the assassination. This document, dated Nov. 22, 1963, is the same day I was assigned, for a second time, the job of locating Milteer. My superior Royal McGraw knew I was going out to search for Milteer; he told me at the time that he had no idea where Milteer was.

McGraw knew I went to Quitman, to Valdosta and to all of Milteer's known haunts to locate him as ordered. McGraw knew that I (and others) looked for Milteer that afternoon and evening and in the days that followed until I finally tracked Milteer down late Wednesday, Nov. 27. McGraw knew the status of my assignment; he knew, by radio, the minute I found Milteer. He had known all along that Milteer was not in Valdosta or Quitman, nor did he have any information as to the whereabouts of Milteer. Yet, documents say that *someone* told the Atlanta office that Milteer was in Quitman at the time of the assassination. By providing false information, somebody essentially gave an alibi to a suspect known to have planned to kill the president.

Taken even further, this statement – and later alibis for Milteer – must have had an impact on the reception of my written report once I had found and interviewed Milteer. Finally, it also underscores the limited line of questioning I was ordered to follow once Milteer was located. There was *no* reason to question Milteer

FEDERAL BUREAU OF INVESTIGATION
U. S. DEPARTMENT OF JUSTICE
COMMUNICATIONS SECTION

NOV 22 1963

TELETYPE

REC-3

| Mr. Tolson |
| Mr. Belmont ✓ |
| Mr. Mohr |
| Mr. Casper |
| Mr. Callahan |
| Mr. Conrad |
| Mr. DeLoach |
| Mr. Evans |
| Mr. Gale |
| Mr. Rosen ✓ |
| Mr. Sullivan |
| Mr. Tavel |
| Mr. Trotter |
| Tele. Room |
| Miss Holmes |
| Miss Gandy |

URGENT 11/22/63 5-43PM EST LG

TO DIRECTOR, AND SAC-S DALLAS, AND MIAMI

FROM SAC, ATLANTA /89-44/ 1P

ASSASSINATION OF PRESIDENT KENNEDY, NOVEMBER TWENTY SECOND

SIXTY THREE.

RE MIAMI AIRTEL TO BUREAU NOV. TWELVE LAST, CAPTIONED

THREAT TO KILL PRES. KENNEDY BY J. A. MILTEER AT MIAMI, FLA.,

NOV. NINE LAST.

MILTEER-S WHEREABOUTS AT QUITMAN, GA., THIS DATE ASCERTAINED

AND SECRET SERVICE ADVISED. LOCAL SECRET SERVICE ALSO ADVISED

OF WHEREABOUTS OF J. B. STONER, BOMB SUSPECT, AND MELVIN BRUCE,

WHO WAS INVOLVED IN RIOTS OXFORD, MISSISSIPPI, DURING DESEGREGATION

OF UNIVERSITY OF MISS.

END ACK

WA 5-47 PM OK FBI WA WS

DL 4-45 PM

MM 5-45 PM OK FBI MM CS

TU DISC

REC-8 2-109060

25 DEC 1963

MR. BELMONT FOR THE DIRECTOR

MR. ROSEN

This FBI teletype dated Nov. 22, 1963 (and time-stamped just over five hours after President Kennedy was assassinated) fraudulently states that Milteer was in Quitman that day. The teletype was sent by SAC McMahon of the Atlanta FBI Office. Who was the source of the determination that Milteer was Georgia?

at length, since he had been reported – with no real evidence – to have been in Georgia at the time of the assassination!

I knew nothing about this memo at the time. Had I known then – or at any time before the investigation was closed and the Warren Commission report compiled – I would have challenged that report and could have shown this statement to be a fabrication.

This deception about Milteer's whereabouts was not just perpetrated by one person; it touches the Atlanta FBI office and FBI headquarters in Washington, D.C. I have discovered this compounded lie in documents I found in the National Archives – fraudulent documents that are more than just a simple lie about where Milteer was the day of the assassination.

FD 302S AND THE FBI REPORTS OF HARDING & McGRAW

In the everyday work schedule of the FBI agent, one of the most important documents that the agent prepares is the "FD 302." In lieu of a recorded or oral statement made by a subject, suspect or witness, the FD 302 is an item of evidence. The interview of the principal subject is the most critical document, since the subject and what he or she says is the foundation of the entire investigation.

Because it can be used as evidence, the FD 302 must be an exact, correctly written and typed document, detailing the questioning of a subject. If the statements in the FD 302 will not hold up in a court of law, then the remainder of the written material has no legal value.

Among the documents I uncovered at the National Archives were the two reports completed by my fellow FBI agents, Special Agent and supervisor Charles Harding (Atlanta Office) and Special Agent Royal McGraw (Thomasville Office). Harding's report [**Doc. #2**] was dated Dec. 1, 1963. It covered the period from Nov. 22 to Dec. 1, 1963 and listed the case title as Lee Harvey Oswald. McGraw's report [**Doc. #3**] was dated Jan. 22, 1964, covered the period of Jan. 13-14, and had a case title of Joseph Adams Milteer.

Both agents used an FD 302 in their respective reports that detailed a Nov. 27, 1963, interview of Milteer. The FD 302 in

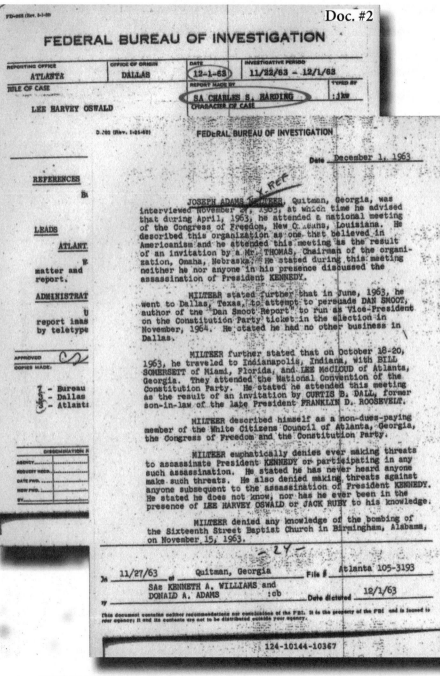

Doc. #2

FD-263 (Rev. 1-1-10)

FEDERAL BUREAU OF INVESTIGATION

REPORTING OFFICE	OFFICE OF ORIGIN	DATE	INVESTIGATIVE PERIOD
ATLANTA	DALLAS	12-1-63	11/22/63 – 12/1/63

TITLE OF CASE	REPORT MADE BY	TYPED BY
LEE HARVEY OSWALD	SA CHARLES S. HARDING	:jkw
	CHARACTER OF CASE	

D-302 (Rev. 1-25-60)   FEDERAL BUREAU OF INVESTIGATION

Date December 1, 1963

REFERENCES

B:

LEADS

ATLANT.

matter and
report.

ADMINISTRAT

report inas
by teletype

APPROVED

COPIES MADE:

7 - Bureau
5 - Dallas
3 - Atlanta

JOSEPH ADAMS MILTEER, Quitman, Georgia, was
interviewed November 9, 1963, at which time he advised
that during April, 1963, he attended a national meeting
of the Congress of Freedom, New Orleans, Louisiana. He
described this organization as one that believed in
Americanism and he attended this meeting as the result
of an invitation by a Mr. THOMAS, Chairman of the organization, Omaha, Nebraska. He stated during this meeting
neither he nor anyone in his presence discussed the
assassination of President KENNEDY.

MILTEER stated further that in June, 1963, he
went to Dallas, Texas, to attempt to persuade DAN SMOOT,
author of the "Dan Smoot Report" to run as Vice-President
on the Constitution Party ticket in the election in
November, 1964. He stated he had no other business in
Dallas.

MILTEER further stated that on October 18-20,
1963, he traveled to Indianapolis, Indiana, with BILL
SOMERSETT of Miami, Florida, and LEE McCLOUD of Atlanta,
Georgia. They attended the National Convention of the
Constitution Party. He stated he attended this meeting
as the result of an invitation by CURTIS B. DALL, former
son-in-law of the late President FRANKLIN D. ROOSEVELT.

MILTEER described himself as a non-dues-paying
member of the White Citizens Council of Atlanta, Georgia,
the Congress of Freedom and the Constitution Party.

MILTEER emphatically denies ever making threats
to assassinate President KENNEDY or participating in any
such assassination. He stated he has never heard anyone
make such threats. He also denied making threats against
anyone subsequent to the assassination of President KENNEDY.
He stated he does not know, nor has he ever been in the
presence of LEE HARVEY OSWALD or JACK RUBY to his knowledge.

MILTEER denied any knowledge of the bombing of
the Sixteenth Street Baptist Church in Birmingham, Alabama,
on November 15, 1963.

DISSEMINATION R		
AGENCY		
REQUEST RECD		
DATE FWD		
HOW FWD		
BY		

On 11/27/63 at Quitman, Georgia   File # Atlanta 105-3193

by SAs KENNETH A. WILLIAMS and
DONALD A. ADAMS   :cb   Date dictated 12/1/63

This document contains neither recommendations nor conclusions of the FBI. It is the property of the FBI and is loaned to
your agency; it and its contents are not to be distributed outside your agency.

124-10144-10367

December 1, 1963, the date of Harding's report, is the same day shown as the accompanying FD 302's
dictation date. The FD 302 states the information was gathered on 11/27/63 by me and another agent.
I turned in my FD 302 on the 28th. Interestingly, many of the suspicious documents about Milteer's
whereabouts are dated between November 27 (the day I actually found Milteer) and December 1, 1963. 63

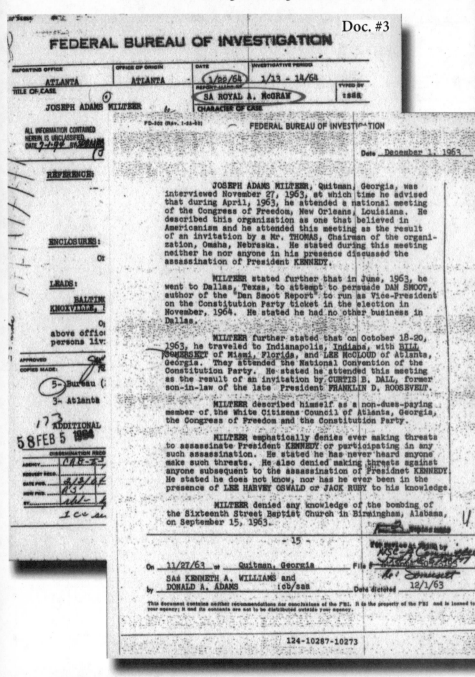

Doc. #3

FEDERAL BUREAU OF INVESTIGATION

REPORTING OFFICE	OFFICE OF ORIGIN	DATE	INVESTIGATIVE PERIOD
ATLANTA	ATLANTA	1/22/64	1/13 - 14/64

TITLE OF CASE
REPORT MADE BY: SA ROYAL A. McGRAW TYPED BY: sas

JOSEPH ADAMS MILTEER

CHARACTER OF CASE

ALL INFORMATION CONTAINED
HEREIN IS UNCLASSIFIED
DATE 2-1-84 BY

REFERENCE:

ENCLOSURES:

LEADS:
BALTIM
KNOXVILLE,

above office
persons liv:

APPROVED
COPIES MADE:
5- Bureau (
3- Atlanta

173 ADDITIONAL
58 FEB 5 1964

FD-302 (Rev. 1-25-60) FEDERAL BUREAU OF INVESTIGATION

Date December 1, 1963

JOSEPH ADAMS MILTEER, Quitman, Georgia, was interviewed November 27, 1963, at which time he advised that during April, 1963, he attended a national meeting of the Congress of Freedom, New Orleans, Louisiana. He described this organization as one that believed in Americanism and he attended this meeting as the result of an invitation by a Mr. THOMAS, Chairman of the organization, Omaha, Nebraska. He stated during this meeting neither he nor anyone in his presence discussed the assassination of President KENNEDY.

MILTEER stated further that in June, 1963, he went to Dallas, Texas, to attempt to persuade DAN SMOOT, author of the "Dan Smoot Report" to run as Vice-President on the Constitution Party ticket in the election in November, 1964. He stated he had no other business in Dallas.

MILTEER further stated that on October 18-20, 1963, he traveled to Indianapolis, Indiana, with BILL SOMERSETT of Miami, Florida, and LEE McCLOUD of Atlanta, Georgia. They attended the National Convention of the Constitution Party. He stated he attended this meeting as the result of an invitation by CURTIS B. DALL, former son-in-law of the late President FRANKLIN D. ROOSEVELT.

MILTEER described himself as a non-dues-paying member of the White Citizens Council of Atlanta, Georgia, the Congress of Freedom and the Constitution Party.

MILTEER emphatically denies ever making threats to assassinate President KENNEDY or participating in any such assassination. He stated he has never heard anyone make such threats. He also denied making threats against anyone subsequent to the assassination of President KENNEDY. He stated he does not know, nor has he ever been in the presence of LEE HARVEY OSWALD or JACK RUBY to his knowledge.

MILTEER denied any knowledge of the bombing of the Sixteenth Street Baptist Church in Birmingham, Alabama, on September 15, 1963.

- 15 -

On	11/27/63	at	Quitman, Georgia	File
SAs	KENNETH A. WILLIAMS and			
by	DONALD A. ADAMS :cb/saa			Date dictated 12/1/63

This document contains neither recommendations nor conclusions of the FBI. It is the property of the FBI and is loaned to your agency; it and its contents are not to be distributed outside your agency.

124-10287-10273

FBI Senior Resident Agent Royal McGraw's Jan. 22, 1964 report also purports to present the FD 302 of my November 27th interview with Milteer. The FD 302s in both Harding's and McGraw's report should be exact duplicates. The most glaring difference is the date in the last paragraph, September 15, 1963. That is the correct date of the bombing in Birmingham. Why was Harding's earlier report wrong?

both reports is fraudulent. The FD 302 used in those reports should be identical. The only allowable difference would be redacted information. Otherwise, the copies should be identical – they have to be to ensure authenticity. On close inspection, the reports are not identical. Check out the spacing on the sides, top and bottom of the pages. But spacing is not the only anomaly.

At the bottom of the FD 302s, the steno's initials are different. In Harding's report the initials are :cb; in McGraw's the initials are shown as :cb/saa. Also note the numbers immediately below the steno initials; in one report the numbers read 124-10287-10273; the other set of numbers is 124-10144-10367. Finally, and perhaps the most glaring difference is the date on the last line of the bottom paragraph in the body of the report. *The dates are different* – September 15, 1963 and November 15, 1963. The September 15 date is the correct one, the "mistake" appears to have crept in when someone altered my original FD 302 information.

If you copy something, the original and the copy should be identical in all aspects. If the documents were identical, then none of the differences described above would be present.

This is far more than carelessness. This is deliberate deception on the part of two veteran FBI agents, both of whom knew better.

FBI Agents Charles Harding and Royal McGraw both submitted a fraudulent FD 302 of my interview of Joseph Adams Milteer and included other data from my reports in their respective reports. When they did that, they essentially made the report a worthless piece of evidence. Had this matter ever gone to court in the prosecution of a subject or subjects, and the altering of my FD 302 surfaced, the case would have been thrown out.

I had begun my interview of Joseph Adams Milteer on Wednesday evening, Nov. 27, 1963, after locating him five days after the assassination. I then interviewed Milteer until the early morning hours of Nov. 28, after which I went back to my residence and wrote my FD 302, and phoned in a teletype to the Atlanta FBI Office. Later that morning, I dictated both to a steno.

More than 40 years later, I found the information from my original FD 302 [**Doc. #4**] in the National Archives; it was loose and included in a folder marked "Milteer." The FD 302 information had been altered and was now presented in the form of a "Letterhead Memorandum " or LHM. The unsigned LHM had the date of November 29, 1963, and no agent attribution. And in the body of the FD 302/LHM, *someone had re-arranged my writings and included, as the first paragraph, a description of things I never asked Milteer about during the questioning.* That entire first paragraph was never seen by me until 44 years later, when I found the loose LHM.

The name of Mr. Thomas in that first paragraph was totally new to me because I didn't discuss him or his being the chairman of the Congress of Freedom with Milteer.

To my best recollection, the second through the sixth paragraphs are correct. They detail the answers to the five (and only five) questions I was ordered to ask Milteer by SAC James McMahon. I did my job, but I am left to wonder all these years later, what actually happened?

In the FD 302s [**Docs. #2 & #3**] displayed in the reports by Harding and McGraw, Special Agent Kenneth Williams was listed above the name of Donald A. Adams. This was in violation of FBI policy. I was the lead investigating agent. I conducted the interview of Milteer. Williams was called by me to help apprehend Milteer. He knew nothing about the reason Milteer was to be questioned until I called on him for help. Williams was merely sitting in on the interview as a witness, nothing more.

In fact, when I wrote my rough draft for the steno to type, my best recollection is that I wrote only my name on the line after "By." If I did write both our names, I know beyond a doubt that I wrote my name first and Williams' name beneath because he never asked one question. If questions were raised later in a court of law, with Williams being listed as the lead investigative agent, he would be the agent called to testify about the report.

In comparing the complete Harding and McGraw reports I realized that not only was some of the data missing, which I had included in my FD 302, but it was inserted into different places, and some things had been altered. For example, the height of

NARA ~~[illegible]~~ DATE 4-21-07

Doc. #4

UNITED STATES DEPARTMENT OF JUSTICE

FEDERAL BUREAU OF INVESTIGATION

In Reply, Please Refer to
File No.

Atlanta, Georgia
November 29, 1963

ASSASSINATION OF PRESIDENT KENNEDY
NOVEMBER 22, 1963, DALLAS, TEXAS

Texas In.l

JOSEPH ADAMS MILTEER, Quitman, Georgia, was interviewed November 27, 1963. MILTEER advised that during
April, 1963, he attended a national meeting of the Congress
of Freedom, New Orleans, Louisiana. He described this
organization as one that believed in Americanism and he
attended this meeting as the result of an invitation by
a Mr. THOMAS, Chairman of the organization, Omaha, Nebraska.
He stated during this meeting neither he nor anyone in his
presence discussed the assassination of President KENNEDY.

never discussed with me

MILTEER stated further that in June, 1963, he
went to Dallas, Texas, to attempt to persuade DAN SMOOT,
author of the "Dan Smoot Report" to run as Vice-President
on the Constitution Party ticket in the election in
November, 1964. He stated he had no other business in Dallas.

rect   *Texas 2.*

MILTEER further stated that on October 18-20,
1963, he traveled to Indianapolis, Indiana, with BILL
SOMERSETT of Miami, Florida, and LEE MC CLOUD of Atlanta,
Georgia. They attended the National Convention of the
Constitution Party. He stated he attended this meeting
as the result of an invitation by CURTIS B. DALL, former
son-in-law of the late President FRANKLIN D. ROOSEVELT.

vrect   *Ga. 2.*   *2nd*

MILTEER described himself as a non-dues-paying
member of the White Citizens Council of Atlanta, Georgia,
The Congress of Freedom and the Constitution Party.

vrect

MILTEER emphatically denies ever making threats
to assassinate President KENNEDY or participating in any
such assassination. He stated he has never heard anyone
make such threats. He also denied making threats against
anyone subsequent to the assassination of President KENNEDY.
He stated he does not know, nor has he ever been in the
presence of LEE HARVEY OSWALD or JACK RUBY to his knowledge.

ct

MILTEER denied any knowledge of the bombing of
the Sixteenth Street Baptist Church in Birmingham, Alabama,
on November 15, 1963.

vrect

~~COPIES DESTROYED~~

4 4 JAN 9 1973

This unsigned Letterhead Memorandum from the Atlanta FBI office dated November 29, 1963
was the earliest representation (I have found) of the statements that showed up later in Harding's and McGraw's report as the purported FD 302 of my Milteer interview. I used the correct
date, Sept. 15, 1963, in my original FD 302 and suspect the date mistake began in Atlanta.

Doc. #5

AT 105-3193
2

MILTEER is described as follows:

Name	JOSEPH ADAMS MILTEER
Date of Birth	February 26, 1902
Place of Birth	Quitman, Georgia
Race	White
Sex	Male
Height	5' 4"
Weight	160 pounds
Eyes	Blue
Hair	Partially thinning and gray
Complexion	Ruddy
Characteristics	Wears glasses with metal frame, heavy waisted, small round shouldered, nearly always unshaven, short gray stubble with about two days growth, shabby dresser, wears old fashioned clothes, hunting type cap, tan in color, short legged, most of height from waist upwards.
Education	Graduate of Quitman, Georgia, High School
Relatives	None known
Automobile	Drives 1962 Volvo, bearing 1963 Georgia tag 61-D-226, gray or tan in color. Also drives unknown year Volkswagen, bearing 1963 Georgia tag 11D2762, believed property of Mrs. C. C. COFIELD, 212 South Troupe Street, Valdosta, Georgia, prostitute with whom MILTEER lives part time.
Arrest Record	Arrested 1955 Valdosta, Georgia, suspicion of burglary and released.

- 25 -

Milteer never told me about the arrest.

68   Harding's Dec. 1, 1963 report contains personal data different from what I had gathered. Milteer's height is listed here as 5' 4", but mine and earlier reports listed his height as 5' 7" or 5' 8".

Milteer was different from what I had noted in my FD 302. I had listed his height as 5'8"; but in both McGraw's and Harding's reports Milteer's height is written as 5'4" [**Doc. #5**].

I know that the FD 302s in both the Harding and the McGraw reports are not mine. Their FD 302s use some information I gathered, but not as I wrote it. Whoever manufactured those reports created fraudulent documents.

HARDING'S REPORT OF DEC. 1, 1963

The Dec. 1, 1963 report of FBI Special Agent Charles S. Harding is titled Lee Harvey Oswald [**Doc. #2**], with the character of the case listed as IS-R, which signifies Internal Security-Russia. This report has become *the* reference document when official investigative bodies examine the questions around Milteer.

This 33-page report, with a field office file number of 105-3193 (available online at maryferrel.org), begins with a synopsis that contains some information from my FD 302s. Portions of Harding's report are included in the documents section of this book.

After the synopsis is my FD 302 on Vereen Alexander [**Doc. #6**]. It is the first document in the "Lee Harvey Oswald" section of the report and contains the information Alexander furnished me when she suddenly appeared at my front door two days after the assassination.

The full report is an odd collection of strange and fantastic accusations about the assassination and some of its main players. Many of these claims are then shown to have been investigated and debunked. Appearing toward the end of a "Miscellaneous" section are three pages concerning Milteer. First there is the fraudulent FD 302 on Milteer attributed to Ken Williams and myself, then the personal data [**Doc. #5**], and another document we will discuss later.

Agents Harding and McGraw must have played an essential part in the altered reports. Harding appears to be the point man for contact with the Secret Service, and McGraw, as the senior resident agent at the Thomasville office, was required to approve and initial any report before it was sent out to the other offices.

FD-302 (Rev. 1-25-60)

FEDERAL BUREAU OF INVESTIGATION

Doc. #6

1

Date _November 26, 1963_

      Miss VEREEN ALEXANDER, 101 Montrose Drive, advised that while she attended Sophie Newcomb College, Girls' Division, Tulane University, New Orleans, Louisiana, she met JOHN BASS, 2225 Jena Street, Apartment C; ED CLARK; AL PECCARERO (phonetic); and LIONEL HAMPTION (last name not certain).

      On an average of once per week during the past year the above group discussed politics at the University Center at Tulane University. On May 23, 1963, the discussion concerned the attempted assassination of President DE GAULLE of France, with the conversation shifting to the question as to how one would go about the assassination of the President. President KENNEDY's name was not mentioned in the discussion.

      Miss ALEXANDER advised that the above listed four individuals have strong Marxist and Pro-Cuban feelings.

      Miss ALEXANDER advised that she, along with ROBERT HOFFMAN, published a newspaper called "The Reed", which she described as "a very liberal paper."

      She advised that ROBERT HOFFMAN's brother, DAVE HOFFMAN, held a party during the summer of 1963 in his apartment near Slogan's Bar in New Orleans. At his party BASS, CLARK, PECCARERO and HAMPTION were present, along with PATTY HAHN, BEN HOGAN and others. Miss ALEXANDER had the strong belief that LEE HARVEY OSWALD was also possibly present at this party.

      She stated that PECCARERO is a leader or a member of a local Socialist group in New Orleans.

- 4 -

On _11/25/63_ at _Thomasville, Georgia_   File # _Atlanta 105-3193_

by _SA DONALD A. ADAMS /evg/hld_   Date dictated _11/25/63_

Harding's Dec. 1, 1963 report contains as page four my FD 302 on Vereen Alexander. I wrote and dictated it on the same day, Monday November 25, 1963.

McGraw's Report of Jan. 22, 1964

Doctor Jeff Caufield, who is writing a book on Joseph Adams Milteer, made available to me a report prepared by FBI Special Agent Royal A. McGraw, dated Jan. 22, 1964 two months after the assassination of President Kennedy [**Doc. #3**]. The "Character of the Case" is listed as "Racial Matters." It should have been classified under "The Assassination of President John F. Kennedy." Any Bureau office receiving the report would file it as stated. The complete report is available in the documents section of this book.

McGraw was one of the best report writers in the Bureau. He was so recognized by superiors, his associates and me. When McGraw wrote that the character of the case was Racial Matters, he may have done this intentionally. No one would look in the Racial Matters Section for evidence involving threats to assassinate JFK. In my opinion this entire report was generated to whitewash (Milteer) and his involvement in those threats. Among the discrepancies I want to note for the reader are:

1. The actual FD 302 of my Nov. 27, 1963, interview of Milteer is missing. I had prepared a complete report on my investigation and called it in to the Atlanta FBI Office.

2. The descriptive data in my supposed FD 302 report contained additional information beyond what I had obtained from Milteer when I interviewed him. I know what I asked and what I wrote, and this is not the FD 302 I produced.

3. As mentioned before, the entire first paragraph of Milteer's 302 was not anything that I discussed with him, and I am not familiar with what was written there.

4. McGraw's report states, "Milteer was photographed by FBI agents on November 27, 1963, and copies of this photograph are maintained by Atlanta." This is the first notice given that the FBI had a picture of Milteer, since the Secret Service first asked for one, over a week before the assassination.

Where did this photograph come from? I never had an occasion to photograph Milteer, and had never sent any photograph. Milteer was in my control on that date and neither I nor Agent Williams took any photos of Milteer. I had only asked the five questions I had been tasked to do. The photo of Milteer is as clear a likeness as I've ever seen, but lists his height incorrectly as 5'5". The date written on the reverse of the photo says it was "taken 11/27/63," which was the date of my interview of Milteer, but it is not in my handwriting nor any that is familiar to me. This photo was first mentioned in McGraw's report of Jan. 22, 1964. Why did it take so long?

5. The bottom three lines of McGraw's report synopsis read: "Milteer reportedly carries a .38 caliber revolver in his car when traveling and caution should be used in event Milteer is contacted." This was written in capital letters and underlined, which is the procedure used by all FBI agents to ensure that the caution statement is read by every agent who reads this report or has any dealings with the relevant subject. McGraw included this information in his report, yet he never told me about it, nor did he caution me to be careful of Milteer. He placed my life and the life of Agent Ken Williams in jeopardy when he kept this information to himself. He violated what all FBI agents are taught to recognize as "Priority Number One."

6. On Page two, McGraw writes that "Milteer on Nov. 27, 1963 advised etc." Everyone in the Bureau who writes reports and every steno who prepares the final copy would know

from this that McGraw did not interview Milteer and that he intentionally failed to name the person who did. Had he followed proper procedure and named the interviewer, many people would have questioned the report.

7. The report also details the record checks that were made at Quitman, Georgia, on Sept. 24, 1962. This inclusion in the report raises another incorrect and deceptive flag, since the top, right-hand section of the cover page [Doc. #3] provides an area for the investigative period. All FBI personnel know that the investigative period is the first date that any investigation or inquiry is made through the last date regarding the matter that is being investigated. Yet McGraw wrote the investigative period as Jan. 13-14, 1964. A most significant piece of information in this report shows that Chief William Elliott of the Quitman Police Department furnished information to the FBI concerning Milteer on Sept. 24, 1962. If that was the earliest date in the details of the report, then that date should have been the first date in the investigative period. This is the same Bill Elliott that I called on to help me during my first background investigation on Milteer in mid-November 1963, and during all of the time that Elliott and I worked the Milteer investigation, he never mentioned the earlier work at any time. Nor did he mention that McGraw interviewed him about Milteer, nor did McGraw ever let on anything about that 1962 investigation. I can't help but question why both were secretive about this.

As the report progresses, McGraw goes into detail about Milteer's political activities, painting a portrait of a racist misfit who plans to form a new political party that mirrors his radical thinking.

Tucked into the remaining pages, is information that I, in November 1963, knew nothing about: Milteer's visit to Florida on November 9. McGraw wrote: "Milteer talked about plans in the making to kill President Kennedy at some future date," that Milteer had suggested Jack Brown, from Chattanooga, Tennessee, as someone "who could do the job," and that Milteer was familiar with Washington and "would be willing to help."

In McGraw's report, he combines multiple threats against the president as if they had all occurred in Miami on Nov. 9, 1963.

But the information about the Washington threat came from the October meeting in Indianapolis with Milteer, the informant and others. That was what I supposedly had been sent to investigate in mid-November.

Additionally, McGraw's report contains the information from Somersett that Milteer was jubilant over the death of President Kennedy, stating that "everything ran true to form. I guess you thought I was kidding you when I said he would be killed from a window with a high-powered rifle."

Why, from a report writer as exceptional as McGraw, was this information buried in a report characterized as Racial Matters and not brought to the forefront of the JFK assassination investigation? What could possibly have been the motive for such deception? Had there been an ongoing cover-up to ensure that no one other than the murdered Lee Harvey Oswald would be considered in an official investigation?

U.S. Secret Service report November 22-25, 1963

The U.S. Secret Service document [**Doc. #7**] from the Atlanta office is perhaps the most fraudulent of those I researched. Written on Nov. 27, the report is titled "Alleged Possible Threat Against the President" and covers the period from Nov. 22 to Nov. 25, 1963. It is checking on three potentially dangerous persons immediately following the assassination. One of those three persons was Joseph Adams Milteer.

Midway down the first page of that report, it reads:

> FBI Agent Charles Harding contacted their Agent at Thomasville who immediately ascertained that *J.A. Milteer was in Quitman at the time of the assassination* [emphasis added].

This as we know is a lie. I was searching for and did not find Milteer until late Nov. 27, 1963. Who was the FBI's "Agent" in Thomasville? It had to have been Royal McGraw, he was the only other agent in Thomasville. If he found him, why didn't he tell me? Why didn't McGraw ask Milteer the five questions?

Doc. #7

RELEASED PER P.L. 102-526 (JFK ACT)
NARA _____ DATE 6-17-94

REPRODUCED AT THE NATIONAL ARCHIVES

ORIGIN Chief's Office	OFFICE Atlanta, Ga.		FILE NO. CO-2-33,915
TYPE OF CASE Protective Research	STATUS Continued		TITLE OR CAPTION X-3-11-5563-S
INVESTIGATION MADE AT Atlanta, Ga.	PERIOD COVERED 11-22-63 - 11-25-63		Alleged Possible Threat Against the President –
INVESTIGATION MADE BY SAIC A. D. Wentz			Joseph Adams Milteer
DETAILS			Lee McCloud
			Jessie Benjamin Stoner

SYNOPSIS

Check on potentially dangerous
persons November 22-25, 1963.
All accounted for. PRS so advised.

DETAILS OF INVESTIGATION

Immediately after learning of the President's assassination at Dallas we began
ascertaining the whereabouts of known subjects who might be suspected.

Capt. R. B. Little, Intelligence Division, Atlanta Police Department, had seen
J. B. Stoner in Atlanta one hour before the assassination. He is, we feel, the
most likely of the group to do something drastic.

FBI Agent Charles Harding contacted their Agent at Thomasville who immediately
ascertained that J. A. Milteer was in Quitman at the time of assassination.

We also learned that Lee McCloud was in Atlanta.

Herbert Wallace Butterworth, according to FBI Agent Harding, was in Philadelphia
at the time and was under surveillance. They continued surveillance until after
the funeral on November 25.

Olga Butterworth, sister of Wallace, was at her home in Wallingford, Pennsylvania.

Inspector Torina called me on November 24 — and a little later SA Holmes from
PRS — requesting that we review files and advise if any dangerous subject might
appear in Washington. I informed them of our previous check.

DISTRIBUTION	COPIES	REPORT MADE BY	DATE
Chief	Orig. & cc		11-27-63
Nashville	1 cc	SPECIAL AGENT In Charge	
Miami	1 cc	APPROVED	DATE
Birmingham	1 cc		
Atlanta	2 cc's	SPECIAL AGENT IN CHARGE	

(CONTINUE ON PLAIN PAPER)

---

repeat copy

2.
CO-2-33,915
X 3-11-5563-S

On Monday morning, the 25th, with the help of Capt. Little and FBI Agent Harding,
we again determined that all the above-named subjects were accounted for locally
and in Pennsylvania.

In my M/R of 11-14-63 I stated we would try to obtain a photograph of J. A.
Milteer. Thus far we have been unable to do so.

I am continuing the case and if we can find one, we will forward it to you.

UNDEVELOPED LEADS

The President was assassinated on Friday the 22nd, Oswald was murdered on Sunday the 24th. This report covers actions to see where certain persons were during that time period. Did Harding's assertion of Milteer's whereabouts come from the same source as that in the FBI Teletype of Nov. 22 [Doc.#1]?

The second page of this report, written by FBI SAIC A.B. Wentz of the Atlanta office says:

> *On Monday morning, the 25th, with the help of Capt. Little and FBI Agent Harding, we again determined that all the above-named subjects were accounted for locally* and in Pennsylvania [emphasis added].

Again, why the deception? I did not locate Milteer in Georgia until late Wednesday the 27th.

A question that needs answering is whether Harding actually talked with anyone in Thomasville, and if he did, who was it? If Harding didn't talk to an agent in Thomasville, what would be his motive for the deception. And why would he and/or McGraw lie about the location of a suspect known to be a potential threat to the president?

Rowse Memorandum

Another fraudulent document is a Letterhead Memorandum (LHM) titled "Assassination of President Kennedy, AFO" (Assaulting Federal Officer), dated Nov. 27, 1963, from Atlanta FBI Field Office Supervisor Henry G. Rowse Jr. [**Doc. #8**] This document suggests deliberate fabrication of information and statements on the part of FBI supervisors that they must have known to be totally false.

This document says FBI Headquarters Section Chief C.L. McGowan, Civil Rights Section in Washington, D.C., telephoned Atlanta SAC James McMahon advising him that J.A. Milteer, of Quitman, Georgia, should be interviewed regarding the assassination of President John F. Kennedy. The LHM references earlier Miami and Atlanta teletypes of Nov. 26, 1963. In addition, McGowan requested Milteer's long-distance telephone records be checked to see if any calls were made to Dallas or New Orleans during the pertinent period.

The second paragraph of this memorandum reads:

> *This information was telephonically furnished to SA Donald A. Adams.* He was advised to contact SA Kenneth Williams and

Doc. #8

OPTIONAL FORM NO. 12
MAY 1962 EDITION
GSA GEN. REG. NO. 27

UNITED STATES GOVERNMENT

Memorandum

TO : SAC, ATLANTA (89-45)　　　　　DATE: 11/27/63

FROM : HENRY G. ROWSE, JR.

SUBJECT: ASSASSINATION OF PRESIDENT KENNEDY
AFO

　　　　At 2:50 p.m. 11/27/63, Section Chief C. L.
MC GOWAN, Civil Rights Section, telephonically contacted
SAC JAMES E. McMAHON and advised that the Bureau desires
to have J. A. MILTEER, Quitman, Georgia, interviewed
concerning captioned matter in reference to Miami and
Atlanta teletypes, both 11/26/63. Mr. MC GOWAN also
requested to have MILTEER's long distance telephone calls
checked to ascertain if there were any calls to Dallas or
New Orleans during pertinent period.

　　　　This information was telephonically furnished
to SA DONALD A. ADAMS. He was advised to contact SA KENNETH
A. WILLIAMS and furnish him this information and for both
Agents to interview MILTEER inasmuch as SA MC GRAW was on
Annual Leave.

ALL INFORMATION CONTAINED
HEREIN IS UNCLASSIFIED
DATE 9-21-93 BY 9803 RDD/KSR

JFK

2-Atlanta
HGR:elt
(2)

89-45-37

SEARCHED_____INDEXED
SERIALIZED_____FILED
NOV 27 1963
FBI — ATLANTA

124-10260-10346

This is a most interesting document. I could not believe it when researcher Deanne Richards first showed it to me. As I wrote on it, this LHM is "an outright lie as I never received such a call – block stamp initials not my writing." Also, the document shows me signing it in Atlanta on November 27, 1963 – I was in southern Georgia all that day.

to furnish him with this information and for both agents to interview Milteer in as much *as SA McGraw was on annual leave* [emphasis added].

In the lower, right-hand corner is a block stamp dated Nov. 27, 1963 with the name Adams written in the stamp and the initials DAA alongside the name.

This particular document was shown to me in 1994 by JFK researcher Deanie Richards. It was the first time I ever saw it.

This entire document is fraudulent. Not only had I never seen it until 1994, but I knew nothing about it. I was not called as is stated in the second paragraph, and I did not initial it as is shown.

This document, prepared in the Atlanta FBI Office by Rowse, had to be to protect himself, Section Chief McGowan, SAC James McMahon, SA Kenneth Williams and SA Royal McGraw. SAC McMahon's initials are located just below the text on the right-hand side, and Rowse's initials are just below the copy count on the left-hand side at the bottom.

The memo reads as if – after the assassination – this was the order given to me for locating and interviewing Milteer. But as I detail in the Prologue, it was on the afternoon of Nov. 22, 1963, just after the President was assassinated, when I was instructed to call SAC McMahon. It was then, not five days later, that I was instructed to locate Milteer for the Secret Service and ask the five questions. It was then that I started my search for Milteer, checking on his whereabouts three times a day until I finally saw his Volkswagen bus parked at C.C. Cofield's house in Valdosta, Georgia, late on Wednesday the 27th.

The other obvious fabrication was the instruction that I was to contact SA Williams as a back-up agent and that we were both to interview Milteer. I had only contacted Williams as a back-up agent when I found Milteer's vehicle, and Williams appeared to know nothing about the investigation I was conducting.

Finally, why was Royal McGraw described in this memorandum as being "on annual leave?" As he was my only partner in Thomasville, I would have known that he was on annual leave. He was not. We were in daily contact, either in person, or by phone or radio.

FD 302 by Special Agent Kenneth Williams

While going through the documents in the National Archives, I came across one that totally surprised me. It was an FD 302 [**Doc. #9**] said to be written by Kenneth A. Williams on Nov. 27, 1963, the day he assisted me in chasing down Milteer and witnessed my interview. The report was dictated on Dec. 1, the same date as Harding's report, which includes this report plus the suspicious FD 302 on Milteer.

Keep in mind that Williams and I met up about 5:30 P.M., well after work hours, on Nov. 27, 1963. Only then did Williams learn that I had been searching for Milteer for the previous five days and had just located his vehicle. I am convinced that Williams had no knowledge of my investigation. In fact, it was only after I explained why I was involved with the happenings in the Kennedy assassination that he understood why we were pursuing Milteer.

Williams remained with me during the entire time we spent locating, interviewing and taking Milteer into protective custody for the Secret Service, until long after midnight, when we finally completed our interview with Milteer and watched him walk out of the Federal Building in Valdosta, Georgia.

This FD 302 indicates that on Nov. 27, 1963, a Kermit Faulk of Southern Bell Telephone Co. in Valdosta, Georgia, provided Williams with information concerning three telephone calls to Florida, two of them to William Somersett. The calls were made from the telephone listed to C.C. Cofield (Milteer's girlfriend) in Valdosta, Georgia.

I do not know when Williams made this inquiry. From the time I called him to assist with the apprehension of Milteer, Williams was with me and remained in my presence until the early morning hours of the next day. The only time he could possibly have made the inquiry of Mr. Faulk would have been in the hours before we met at 5:30 P.M. I was honest with Ken about what we were going to do, so why would he not tell me that he was making inquiries about phone calls made by Milteer?

If Williams did the work sometime after he left me on the morning of Nov. 28, he was deceptive about the date.

RELEASED PER P.L. 102-526(JFK ACT)
NARA _____ DATE 4/21/07

Doc. #9

-302 (Rev. 1-25-60)

FEDERAL BUREAU OF INVESTIGATION

Date _____ December 1, 1963

      Mr. KERMIT FAULK, Assistant Manager, Southern Bell Telephone and Telegraph Company, Valdosta, Georgia, advised that JOSEPH ADAMS MILTEER has no telephone in Quitman, Georgia.

      Mr. FAULK advised after a check of the toll calls of the telephone listed to Mrs. C. C. COFIELD, Valdosta, Georgia, with whom MILTEER resides part time, that for the period August 26 to November 6, 1963, three calls were made to Miami, Florida, two to WILLIAM SOMERSETT and one to Miami telephone number 371-1031.

-26-

11/27/63 at	Valdosta, Georgia	File # Atlanta 105-3193
SA KENNETH A. WILLIAMS :cb		Date dictated 12/1/63

This document contains neither recommendations nor conclusions of the FBI. It is the property of the FBI and is loaned to

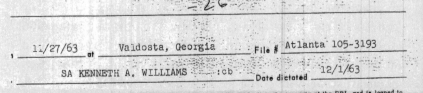

Another suspicious document created between November 27th and December 1st. I had gathered and turned in this same information during my first investigation into Milteer. Notice, the Rowse memo [Doc. #8] asked to check for any calls to Dallas or New Orleans, and here Williams is reporting on calls made to Miami from a period weeks before the assassination.

I had made the same inquiries and had the same information, and it was different from what Rowse requested. In hindsight, I suspect my earlier documents were destroyed, including the phone checks.

It is also puzzling why the file number on Williams' FD 302 is different from the file number on Supervisor Henry G. Rowse's memo, where the alleged request was made. Rowse's memo had the Atlanta file number 89-45; Williams' FD 302 showed the file number 105-3193, which is the number used on Harding's report. If Williams had done as was asked in Rowse's memo, then – as was drilled into every agent's head – he would have used that same file number, not a different one.

Add to that the question of why it took Williams three days to dictate his information to the stenographer. If Rowse's memo was such a priority, given that Section Chief McGowan in Washington had phoned the Atlanta office to request the work, Williams would not have waited three days to complete the assignment. And interestingly, those dates are in accord with the altered FD 302s and other suspect documents, which makes the whole misrepresentation of my investigative accounts appear to be deliberate manipulation. But by whom? And why?

U.S. Secret Service reports November 11-13, 1963

Two Secret Service reports from before the assassination also deserve some scrutiny. The case label is "Protective Research," the same case label as the Secret Service report of Nov. 22, 1963 [**Doc. #7**], which included the claim that Milteer was in Georgia on the assassination day.

The first report [**Doc. #10**] comes from Miami, written by SA Robert Jamison on Nov. 12. The report is titled, "Alleged Possible Threat Against The President," and concerns the November 9, 1963 taped conversation where Milteer discusses shooting the president. Why hadn't I been told of this taped threat when given my assignment on Nov. 13th?

The second two-page report [**Docs. #11A & 11B**] originates in Atlanta, and was written by Agents Wentz and Quim. It is a

Doc. #10

Form No. 1588 (Revised)
MEMORANDUM REPORT
(7-1-30)

VIA AIR MAIL

UNITED STATES SECRET SERVICE
TREASURY DEPARTMENT

Confidential

Dallas - PRS
Function

ORIGIN	Field	OFFICE	Miami, Florida		FILE NO. 3-11-5563-S
TYPE OF CASE		STATUS		TITLE OR CAPTION	
Protective Research		Closed - Miami		Alleged Possible Threat Against	
INVESTIGATION MADE AT			PERIOD COVERED	The President	
Miami, Florida			11-12-63		
INVESTIGATION MADE BY					
SA Robert J. Jamison					

DETAILS

SYNOPSIS

Transcript of conversation involving alleged threat against the President furnished by 3-11-17 copies of which are being furnished the appropriate offices for discreet background checks and photographs of the individuals involved to be obtained through the respective FBI offices. This matter has been classified as "Confidential" by SAIC Bouck.

File no?

DETAILS OF INVESTIGATION

On 11-12-63 informant 3-11-17 furnished this service with a typewritten transcript of recorded conversation between a trusted confidential informant of 3-11-17 and one J.A. Milteer, 212 S. Troupe St., Valdosta, Ga., telephone Cherry 4-1357, with a Post Office Box located at Quitman, Ga. where this individual had run for a political office. This conversation took place on the morning of 11-9-63.

The contents of this transcribed conversation was telephonically furnished to SAIC Bouck, Chief's Office, Washington, D.C. by SA Jamison on 11-12-63. Copies of same attached to the original of this report as well as to the copies of this report being sent to the appropriate offices listed under "Distribution".

SA Jamison conferred personally with SA Leonard Peterson, FBI, Miami, Fla. and Sgt. C.H. Sapp, Commanding Officer, Intelligence, Miami Police Dept., Miami, Fla. re any knowledge of the individuals mentioned in the transcript of the conversation involved and the following information was obtained:

J.A. Milteer, white, male, 48 to 52; 5'7"; 155; glasses; brown graying hair; was last seen driving a white Volkswagon sedan, state and tag number unknown;

DISTRIBUTION	COPIES	REPORT MADE BY		DATE
Chief	Orig.			
Miami	2cc			
SAIC Bouck	2cc	SPECIAL AGENT Robert J. Jamison		11-12-63
Denver	2cc	APPROVED		DATE
Birmingham	2cc			
Atlanta	2cc			
Nashville	2cc	SPECIAL AGENT IN CHARGE John A. Marshall		11-12-63

RJJ RA

JFK Exhibit # 76

This Nov. 12, 1963 Secret Service report concerns a transcript of a recorded conversation made three days earlier on Nov. 9, between a trusted confidential informant identified as "3-11-17" (William Somersett) and "one J. A. Milteer." The report deals with an alleged possible threat by Milteer against the President. I should have been told about this on Nov. 13, when I was assigned to gather information on Milteer.

82

Doc. #11A

Form No. 1790 (Revised)
MEMORANDUM REPORT
(5-1-63)

UNITED STATES SECRET SERVICE
TREASURY DEPARTMENT

FK# 009914

CO-2-33,915

FILE NO. X 3-11-5563-S

ORIGIN	Chief's Office	OFFICE	Atlanta, Ga.	

TYPE OF CASE	STATUS	TITLE OR CAPTION
Protective Research	Continued	Alleged Possible Threat Against the President –

INVESTIGATION MADE AT	PERIOD COVERED	Joseph Adams Milteer
Atlanta, Ga.	11-13-63 – 11-14-63	

INVESTIGATION MADE BY	Lee McCloud
SAIC A. B. Wentz and Special Agent Richard C. Quinn	Jessie Benjamin Stoner

DETAILS

SYNOPSIS

Photographs of Joseph Adams Milteer and Lee McCloud unavailable. Photograph of Jessie Benjamin (J. B.) Stoner, Atlanta Attorney, attached to PRS.

DETAILS OF INVESTIGATION

In report of 11-12-63 SA R. J. Jamison requested that we obtain for the Miami office and PRS photographs of and data on Lee McCloud and J. A. Milteer of 212 S. Troupe Street, Valdosta, Georgia.

Atlanta Police Department has no record on either man. SA Charles Harding, FBI, Atlanta, advised that they do not have photographs. Harding knew of Lee McCloud, an Atlanta business man whom they class as an outspoken segregationist, but so far as they know he has never taken any active part in the Klan or White Citizens Council.

J. A. Milteer, mentioned in the report, is Joseph Adams Milteer, born 2-22-02, blue eyes, gray hair, 5-8, 165 pounds. He holds Georgia Driver's License No. 346534, due to expire in 1966. His address with the Department of Public Safety is 304 N. Clay Street, Quitman, Georgia.

Records disclosed he purchased Georgia 1963 license tag 6-D-226 for a 1962 Volvo, Motor No. 141502678, in Richmond County, Augusta, Georgia, 2-26-63.

On August 15, 1963, he purchased Georgia tag No. 11-D-2762 for a 1963 Volvo, Motor No. 1043319.

On the first tag he showed the 304 N. Clay Street address in Quitman; and the last one as 212s. Troupe Street. Valdosta. Georgia. This last tag was pur-

DISTRIBUTION	COPIES	REPORT MADE BY	DATE
Chief	Orig. & cc	*(signature)* A. B. Wentz	11-14-63
Nashville	2 cc's	SPECIAL AGENT in Charge	
Miami	2 cc's	APPROVED	DATE
Birmingham	1 cc		
Atlanta	2 cc's	SPECIAL AGENT IN CHARGE	

CC-2 number To Birmingham on 11/16/63

CONTINUE ON PLAIN PAPER

180-10091-10200

This two-page Nov. 14, 1963 Secret Service report is very telling. Written the day after the Atlanta FBI Office handed me my first assignment to find Milteer, the document lists Milteer's height as 5' 8". On page two SA Harding says that they have no photograph of Milteer, and that "he would call their Agent McGraw stationed in Thomasville, Georgia, and request that he obtain a photograph." Is that the photo on page 72?

X 3-11-5563-S

Doc. #11B

chased at Valdosta, Georgia?

SA Harding stated they made a thorough investigation of Milteer in connection with the National Convention at Indianapolis on October 19, 1963. We ✓
have reports on that meeting in connection with Herbert Wallace Butterworth
and his sister, Olga. Their investigation revealed that Milteer is a very
outspoken-type individual, active in various segregationist organizations.
They can, however, connect him with no action indicating violence. The most
suspicious action on his part, Harding said, was that enroute to Indianapolis
he stopped at Chattanooga, Tennessee and called on Jack Brown, the Klan member
mentioned in various reports. Harding says they consider Brown to be a dangerous
man from bombing standpoints.

Milteer has no criminal record, Harding stated. He has lived at Quitman for
many years, and that is his actual home. Quitman is located some twenty miles
west of Valdosta. Agent Harding stated he would call their Agent McGraw,
stationed at Thomasville, Georgia, and request that he obtain a photograph
if at all possible. McGraw made the initial investigation for FBI.

Lee McCloud lives at 240 Westminster Drive, N. E., Atlanta. He operates the
Atlanta Truck Cushion Rebuilders, apparently from his home address. Records at
the Department of Public Safety reveal that he purchased Georgia 1963 Tag
1-D-15911 for a 1953 Nash Rambler, Motor No. D541638.

Capt. R. E. Little, in charge of the Intelligence Division, Atlanta Police
Department, is highly capable and reliable. We asked him about Milteer and
McCloud. He stated that McCloud first came to his attention in May, 1962,
when he reported to Little that a Bill Thompson who lives next door to him
and works for the FAA in Atlanta was a sex pervert and communist; that he
was having parties in his home attended by both white men and Negro women, and
white women and Negro men; further, that he kept the place under surveillance
and from observation concluded that McCloud was largely correct, insofar as the
mixed parties were concerned.

Capt. Little stated that McCloud is in his opinion a strong segregationist, but
he is not a violent-type person and would not participate, he thinks, in any
illegal activities. Little considers him to be a reputable business man.

Capt. Little stated he first heard of Milteer last week; that an informant
reported that J. B. Stoner, Connie Lynch, Gene Fallow, and "Mill Teer" were
then in Jacksonville where Stoner, an Attorney, was doing some legal work to
activate the KKK in Florida. He knew nothing further regarding Milteer. ✓
Activities of Lynch and Fallow are unknown to us at this time.

Capt. Little further stated that Attorney J. B. Stoner, Atlanta, is a law
partner of Attorney James R. Venable, with offices in the Walter R. Brown
building opposite Fulton County Court House.

180-10091-10200

In page two of this Secret Service report Harding states, "they [FBI Atlanta office] made a thorough investigation of Milteer in connection with the National Convention at Indianapolis on
October 19, 1963," an assignment I didn't turn in until after Nov. 16. What's going on? Also,
Harding states, "McGraw made the initial investigation for FBI." Why was the Atlanta FBI Office
running interference for Milteer and playing such games *before* the assassination?

response to the earlier request from Miami for a photograph of and data about Milteer and others. The report covers the period from Nov. 13 to Nov. 14 and was written on the 14th.

The report on page two says, "SA Harding stated they made a thorough investigation of Milteer in connection with the National Convention in Indianapolis on October 19, 1963;" and "Agent Harding stated he would call their Agent McGraw, stationed in Thomasville, Georgia, and request that he obtain a photograph if at all possible. McGraw made the initial investigation for FBI."

Hmm, I had been called at home on the evening on Nov. 13, by SAC McMahon to investigate Milteer about the events at that convention in Indianapolis, and, here, in a Nov. 14 report, a day later, Agent Harding tells the Secret Service they had "made a thorough investigation," before I had even turned my report in to Atlanta. Harding also says McGraw did the investigation and asks McGraw for a photograph of Milteer. What was going on? What unwitting role did I play in this charade? Did McGraw, Harding and others conspire to muddle Milteer activities? Why? To what end?

Until I read *High Treason* in 1993, I knew nothing about the Miami Police's Nov. 9, 1963 tape recording of Milteer's threat. I find that shocking. I should have been told when the fact-finding mission was assigned to me on Nov. 13. And when I think back about how my hands were essentially tied by SAC McMahon during my post-assassination interview of Milteer, it causes me serious concerns. Why was I not told the details of Somersett's tape recording of Milteer's discussion regarding plans to kill the President of the United States from an office building with a high-powered rifle? That information would certainly have provided the basis for a deeply penetrative and productive interview.

Why was this knowledge not acted on? The odds are I'll never know, and it will always haunt me.

In 1993, when I first saw pictures of Milteer in *High Treason*, I was flabbergasted. I couldn't believe it. Here was someone who had threatened to kill the President of the United States, standing alongside the motorcade route that fateful day in Dallas. What was going on? I had been sent to find Milteer in Georgia the afternoon of the assassination, but didn't locate him until Wednesday the 27th. Was Milteer in Dallas? I'd say, yes!

CHAPTER NINE

What's Going On?

When I was assigned to the Milteer investigation on Nov. 13, 1963, I should have been informed of the threat against the president that was recorded on Nov. 9. I was also told nothing of another Secret Service investigation of Milteer taking place at the same time. It was not until 30 years later, when I read *High Treason*, that I learned any of this.

The Miami Police Department, the FBI and the Secret Service knew about the assassination plots, so why was this not made a priority? Why wasn't Milteer placed on a top threat index and followed in all of his moves between the time the plots were discovered and JFK traveled to Dallas? Why wasn't Somersett, the informant, interrogated to identify all of Milteer's associates, his past and present travel plans, whom he met with, and the dates of any such meetings?

When the FBI turned over my investigative results to the Secret Service a few days before the president's Dallas trip, and when the information from that investigation was combined with the information of the October Indianapolis meeting and the Miami tape recording, why wasn't the president's trip cancelled or at least given seriously enhanced security? Should not those results have sent up a red flag somewhere?

The Secret Service must have believed the October and November threats to be reliable because the president's means of travel was changed during his trip to Florida on Nov. 18, using a helicopter to get JFK to Miami. Why then, less than a week after changing his Florida travel plans, was the president riding in an open convertible along Dallas streets lined with tall buildings?

According to my research, 1962 is the earliest date that the name Milteer surfaces with the FBI. Information from 1962 was interspersed with reports compiled in 1963 and 1964 and then set forth in a final report prepared by McGraw on Jan. 22, 1964. This was a violation of every proper Bureau procedure. Why would McGraw, a seasoned agent who was well versed – if not exceptional – in report writing, take 1962 investigative results and include them in a 1964 report? And why isn't the original 1962 report in the National Archives?

Was the earlier information ever provided to the Miami and Indianapolis offices at any time after those offices became aware of the threats by Milteer and/or later after the tape recording of Nov. 9, 1963? That information should have been sent to those offices according to Bureau rules and procedures. That's what the FBI is all about: investigating material that reaches its agents until they either solve the case or bring the matter to a logical conclusion.

The Miami FBI office should have provided all of the information they had to the Atlanta and Indianapolis offices, and that same exchange of information should have occurred from Indianapolis to the other offices. It is not known is whether the Indianapolis office knew about the private meeting of Milteer, Somersett and others in Indianapolis on Oct. 18-20, 1963. Did Somersett withhold this information and provide it only to his contacts at the Miami Police Department or the FBI after the fact? If that was done, the next question is why it took from Oct. 20 to Nov. 13 for the U.S. Secret Service to request the investigation I was asked to conduct? Or did it? Was I set up by a person (or persons) in the Atlanta FBI Office to participate in some sort of faux investigation?

If there was paperwork or correspondence between the three offices before the tape recording occurred, I have not found it, although it could possibly be buried deeper in the archives.

If Somersett was close with his police contact, he should have told the agent of the planned trip by Milteer to Indianapolis in October 1963. The Miami agent should then have immediately notified the Indianapolis and Atlanta offices. Indianapolis should have put into motion all that was necessary to cover that meeting and to help Somersett by gathering supporting evidence or additional information. Atlanta should have been requested to obtain all background data about Milteer and forward it to Indianapolis and Miami. Somersett should have provided the details of the meeting, most especially the two plans for assassinating the president, to his local contact immediately upon his return to Miami. Conversely, all information known to the Indianapolis office should have been provided to Miami, Atlanta and other interested offices. Additionally, all communications in this matter should have been sent directly to or copied to FBI Headquarters. Leads should have been spelled out as to what we needed to discover about the suspects in question. If this had been done properly, volumes of information would have been acquired in a very brief period of time, which could have led to new leads and new information. That's the way it was done, from the day I left FBI training school until the day I retired, with the single exception of this supremely important case.

An FBI Airtel dated Nov. 13, 1963 [Doc. #12], titled "Threat to Kill President Kennedy by J.A. Milteer, Miami, Fla. 11/9/63," shows this document was sent to "Director," which is FBI Headquarters. This document and others show beyond any doubt that FBI Headquarters, and therefore the FBI's top administrators, including Director Hoover, knew the details of the threat. Though the FBI was not directly responsible for the safety and security of President Kennedy, his assassination is very much the story of what various agencies and bureaus in the federal government failed to do – whether intentionally or unintentionally – contrary to the training and oaths taken by their personnel.

The Secret Service knew of the tape recording of Milteer's conversation with Somersett in which he discusses killing the president from an office building with a high-powered rifle. Why then, did the Secret Service fail to check potential sniper perches along the Dallas motorcade route? Additionally, the route included two dog-leg turns at Dealey Plaza, relegating the president's car "to the pace of a sitting duck." Why was the motorcade allowed to proceed along a route so fraught with potential risk, especially given the known threats against the life of the president?

FBI

Date: 11/13/63

Transmit the following in _____
(Type in plain text or code)

Via ___ AIRTEL ___ AIRMAIL
(Priority or Method of Mailing)

TO: DIRECTOR, FBI

FROM: SAC, MIAMI (157-900) (P)

J. A. MILTEER
RACIAL MATTERS
(OO: ATLANTA)

ALL INFORMATION CONTAINED
~~CLASSIFIED~~
DATE 10-29-93 BY 9803.1090/KSR
(JFK)

    Re Miami teletypes to the Bureau, 11/10 and 11/63 and Miami airtel, 11/12 /63, captioned "THREAT TO KILL PRESIDENT KENNEDY BY J. A. MILTEER, MIAMI, FLA., 11/9/63."

    Enclosed for the Bureau are 4 Xerox copies, for Atlanta 2 copies, and for other Offices 1 copy of a recorded conversation between WILLIAM SOMERSETT, formerly MM 607-C (RAC) and J. A. MILTEER at Miami, Fla., 11/9/63.

    This information must be treated as confidential and is being labeled "OBSCENE" in view of the language used during the conversation between SOMERSETT and MILTEER.

4 - Bureau (Enc-4) (AM) (RM)
   (1 - 66-16458)
2 - Atlanta (Enc-2) (AM) (RM)
1 - Baltimore (Enc-1) (RM) (Info)
1 - Birmingham (Enc-1) (RM) (Info)
1 - Denver (Enc-1) (RM) (Info)
1 - Jacksonville (Enc-1) (RM) (Info)
1 - Knoxville (Enc-1) (RM) (Info)
1 - Savannah (Info) (Enc-1) (RM)
1 - Washington Field (Info) (Enc-1) (RM)
3 - Miami (1-157-900) (1-137-363Sub A) (1-157-New-THREAT TO
LCP:jlt   KILL PRESIDENT KENNEDY)
(16)

Approved: _____ Sent _____ M Per _____
Special Agent in Charge

MM 157-900

    SOMERSETT advised that when MILTEER left Miami, he planned to attend a political rally for Senator GOLDWATER in Ft. Lauderdale, Fla., on the evening of 11/9/63, and then return to his home in Valdosta, Ga. In addition, MILTEER stated he would contact Attorney LEE in Jacksonville, Fla., regarding the preparation of legal papers relating to his new organization.

    All Offices are requested to be alert for additional information regarding MILTEER's plans and to keep the Bureau and interested Offices advised.

    Based on the information available, Miami will prepare a letterhead memorandum regarding the proposed plan by MILTEER to organize the ACP.

This Nov. 13 FBI Airtel originated from the Miami FBI Office, and was sent to Director, FBI Headquarters, Washington, D.C. This document concerns the recorded conversation of Nov. 9, and confirms that earlier communiques were sent. The Atlanta FBI Office was aware of the threat, but did not tell me, when I was assigned to gather information on Milteer the evening of the 13th. Why?

Did the Secret Service take their responsibilities seriously, and were the agents assigned to the presidential detail qualified for the job? Maybe the agency simply became complacent because nothing like an assassination had happened since President McKinley was shot in 1901. Or was it a case of deliberate neglect?

I know from my days in government that scheduling decisions made by the president and his staff are almost impossible to change. I say "almost impossible" because we do know that previous Miami travel plans for JFK had been changed. I had always thought this change occurred because of the threats made during that Indianapolis meeting, but the authoritative book, *The Secret Service: The Hidden History of an Enigmatic Agency* by Philip Melanson sheds a different light on the subject. He writes that the Miami trip was changed due to a potential threat from Cuban exiles to ram a small plane into Air Force One as it approached the airport for a landing. If this is the reason for the change of plans in Miami, then wasn't that same threat viable with Air Force One flying into Texas a week later?

There is also the dichotomy between the insistence of the Warren Commission Report of Oswald as the lone-gunman and the beliefs of several agents in the presidential detail. There were those who were convinced that the assassination was a conspiracy, and that there was more than one shooter. The widow of agent Roy Kellerman stated that both her husband and fellow agent William Greer – both of whom were in the front seat of the limousine – asserted that there was more to the assassination than the "official" version released to the public.

I want to believe that a complete, thorough, authentic investigation of that crime would have been possible had the law enforcement officials, from the Dallas Police Department to the FBI, been able to do their jobs without interference. With all the evidence available, I know for sure that the investigators would have been able to determine what actually happened, as well as who may have been behind the scenes calling the shots.

The information received by the Miami Police Department and then the Secret Service and the FBI in October and November of 1963 certainly should have set the foundation for a properly completed investigation. It was Nov. 9, 1963, when both the Miami FBI office and the Secret Service obtained a copy of the tape from Lt. Everett Kay of the Miami Police Department's Intelligence Unit of a conversation between Somersett and Milteer where Milteer openly discusses the planned killing of President Kennedy with a high-powered rifle from an office building.

All hell should have broken loose at that moment.

Proper action appears to have been initially taken in Miami, but from there everything fell apart. Nothing was handled correctly, either by the FBI or the Secret Service. The failure to act had to have been deliberate, some working together and others working separately, yet all with the same goal ... the death of JFK.

How High Did the Fraud Go?

Of the many questions I have about the handling of the JFK assassination investigation, one of the most important is: Did FBI Director Hoover know in advance that the assassination was going to happen and fail to act to prevent it from happening? If that was not the case and, for some inexplicable reason, Hoover had been kept in the dark, then why, after the assassination, when he had the information given by William Somersett and others, did he steer the investigation to the lone-gunman conclusion?

There are various books and articles that speculate on just those questions. It is my personal belief, through a review of my history with this case, that Hoover obstructed the truth.

We have been told there were actually at least five separate plans to assassinate President Kennedy, and all of them were put into motion within three to four weeks before Nov. 22, 1963. Separate and most important of all for my understanding was the Miami Police Intelligence Unit tape-recorded conversation from Nov. 9, 1963, during which Joseph Adams Milteer tells his boyhood friend William Somersett (an informant for the Miami Police Intelligence Unit) that they "were going to kill the President with a high-powered rifle from an office building." In the recording, Somersett asked Milteer if his information was correct. Milteer replied that, "It is in the works." Milteer then goes on to say that there will be an arrest right after the shooting to mislead the public.

The Miami Intelligence Unit notified the FBI and the Secret Service immediately. The Washington, D.C. FBI office and others throughout the country were notified about this serious threat. It would seem to go without saying that Director Hoover would have been notified instantly.

As I have said, I did not know of the Nov. 9, 1963 tape recording until 1993, when I read about it in *High Treason*. Here I am, the case agent of the investigation involving Milteer, and I am never informed by anyone in the FBI about the tape recording or the direct threat. Obviously, this information was purposefully kept from me in total violation of the strictest Bureau rules.

While I never knew of the tape recording, my fellow agent and partner Royal McGraw did. It wasn't until 2007 when I discovered his full Jan. 22, 1964 report in the National Archives that I learned that McGraw had been aware of the tape recording.

In hindsight, I started to wonder why I was assigned this most important investigation by SAC McMahon on Nov. 13, 1963. I was an FBI neophyte, a first-office agent. My supervisor in Thomasville, McGraw, had been an agent for 10 years at that time. Could McGraw have made sure the Milteer investigation was assigned to me to give him cover, should any aspect of the Nov. 9 tape-recorded threat become reality?

Another important piece of information kept from me was the earlier investigation conducted in 1962 by McGraw and Quitman Chief of Police Bill Elliott. That investigation was conducted under a case titled "Racial Matters." That would have put McGraw directly in line to carry on with another investigation, only changing the character of the case from "Racial Matters" to "Threats to Kill The President" and then later "The Assassination of President Kennedy." That should and would have been the case if Bureau procedures had been followed. In this case, an exception was made in violation of standard operating procedure, and that exception placed me right in the middle of something I still do not totally understand.

Finally, it has always puzzled me why SAC McMahon ordered me to ask five – and only five – questions of Milteer after the assassination. I remembered how strongly I disagreed with him and how I couldn't understand why he vehemently tied my hands. To this day, I can't help but wonder why he ordered me to do this and whether, had I been free to pursue other lines of questioning, I could have discovered information that might have led to the truth.

In addition to all of the above, I keep remembering how I was cautioned by fellow agents after my transfer to Dallas to keep my opinions about the assassination to myself, and about the destruction of Oswald's note to Agent James Hosty: a note delivered by Oswald in the days before the assassination and later destroyed on orders of SAC Shanklin.

Was it simply President Johnson's paranoia over a Communist conspiracy, whether national or international, and what a nuclear exchange would do to this country, let alone the presidency he had assumed, that made him insist that Oswald was the lone assassin? Was he in collusion with his friend J. Edgar Hoover? Did they decide it didn't matter who killed JFK? With Kennedy gone, Johnson need not fear being replaced as vice president in the 1964 election, and he could then retain the highest office in the land, which he felt he deserved and had earned. Hoover's perspective was much the same: his job would be safe under the presidency of his friend LBJ, since the threat of Hoover's being retired by President Kennedy had disappeared.

Or was it even more nefarious than that? Was there an entire network of people, in and out of government, with motives of profit and power that came together in a perfect storm of a plot to perpetrate the crime of the century – the murder of our 35th president? The planning, organization, precision and operation of a plot of this magnitude boggles the mind, but it could have happened – it could have been pulled off.

I don't know that we will ever know the full truth behind this murder. Neither do I know if we will ever learn for certain just how big a conspiracy it was. I do know that nothing of this scope could have been achieved without some involvement by the man who controlled information flow and the hunt for criminals nationally: FBI Director J. Edgar Hoover.

THE RADICAL RACIST

As you know my ties to the JFK assassination started in 1963 with a resident of Quitman, Georgia, named Joseph Adams Milteer. To review and expand:

Milteer, a right-wing radical, a racist, was a member of the White Citizens Council of Atlanta, Georgia, the Congress of Freedom and the Constitution Party. He didn't work for a living, having inherited some money when his father died, and was described as an outspoken segregationist who passed out hate literature on the street to anyone who would take it. He made no secret of the fact that he hated the Kennedys.

I was a resident agent in southern Georgia, and was called at home one evening and assigned to do a background investigation. That call came from Jim McMahon, the Special Agent in Charge of the Atlanta FBI Office, on Nov. 13, 1963. McMahon told me that Miami Police Department informant William Somersett revealed the details of a plot in which Milteer and three others (including Somersett) talked about killing President Kennedy as he was riding in a motorcade from Homestead Air Force base in Florida to the Kennedy compound in Palm Beach. Part of the discussion included a back-up plan should the first plan fail: to kill the president with a high-powered rifle from a building in Washington, D.C., across from the White House. This plot was discussed in a private meeting among the four at the Constitution Party's gathering in Indianapolis, Indiana, sometime during Oct. 18-20, 1963.

On Nov. 9, 1963, a completely different threat on the president's life was made in a tape-recorded conversation between Milteer and Somersett that took place in Somersett's Miami apartment. This time, Milteer talked about killing President Kennedy with a high-powered rifle from a tall building, after which someone would be arrested for the assassination to divert attention from the real assassin.

Milteer surfaces again with respect to the JFK assassination on the morning of Nov. 22, 1963. According to informant Somersett, Milteer reached him in Miami by phone at 10:30 A.M. that day. Somersett reported that Milteer said he was in Dallas; that the President was coming to Dallas that day; and that the President would never be in Miami again. A June 5, 1968 memorandum [**Doc. #13**] indicates that after receiving this call, Somersett placed calls to two different contacts he had with the Intelligence Division of the Miami Police Department, Captain Charlie Sapp and Sergeant Everett Kay. According to the memorandum:

> Unfortunately, Mr. Sapp was asleep and Mr. Somersett did not ask his wife to wake him. Consequently, he called Sgt. Everett Kay of the Intelligence Division, whose response was, 'It's no use to tell the FBI about this because they won't do anything about it anyway.' Subsequent to the assassination, Somersett did call Sapp back, have him awakened and told him of the various events.

If Milteer called Somersett from Dallas on Nov. 22, 1963, why did investigative officials so willingly believe that Milteer was in Georgia on the day of the President's killing?

Was it because of the information and reports coming from the Atlanta FBI office, such as the Secret Service document [**Doc. #7**], assassination researcher Deanie Richards provided me, asserting that Milteer was in Quitman at the time of the assassination.

That memorandum, written Nov. 27, covers the period from Nov. 22 to Nov. 25, 1963, and deals with the whereabouts of known suspects or persons who had made alleged threats against the President. As noted before, paragraph three of the memorandum reads:

"FBI Agent Charles Harding contacted their Agent at Thomasville [Royal McGraw] who immediately ascertained that J.A. Milteer was in Quitman at the time of assassination."

who is he

Doc. #13

June 5, 1968
Miami, Florida

MEMORANDUM OF CONVERSATION BETWEEN FENSTERWALD AND BILL SOMERSETT

On either November 9th or November 13th, you had a conversation
with Joe Milterr of Valdosta, Georgia. A copy of this memo is
attached. In this conversation, Milterr disclosed to you that he was
trying to organize a new right-wing party and that some of his friends
were not only interested in killing President Kennedy but also Martin
Luther King. This conversation was taped by Intelligence Division
of the Miami Police Dept. and a copy was immediately turned over to
the FBI.

At approximately 10:30 the morning of November 22, 1963, Milterr
called Somersett in Miami. It is concluded that the call was coming
from Dallas, Texas. In essence what Milterr said was "I don't think
you will ever see your boy again in Miami". According to Somersett
on a subsequent occasion, Milterr admitted having made this phone
call to him from Dallas with the above content.

In view of the previous taped conversation, Somersett took the call
from Dallas at face value and placed a call to Mr. Charlie Sapp of
the Intelligence Division. Unfortunately, Mr. Sapp was asleep, and
Mr. Somersett did not ask his wife to wake him. Consequently, he
called Sgt. Everett Kay of the Intelligence Div. whose response was
"it's no use to tell the FBI about this because they won't do anything
about it anyway". Subsequent to the assassination, Somersett did call
Sapp back, have him awakened, and told him of the various events.

Prior to the tapeing of the conversation in early November, Somersett
had been sent on several trips with Milterr. One of these trips was to
Indianapolis where they tried to organize part of the new right-wing
party.

According to Somersett, Milterr had set up in advance an alibi for
this trip to Dallas. He had written a letter to Somersett asking
him to meet with him on the evening of Nov. 24th in Jacksonville.
This letter was apparently written in Valdosta by Milterr on November 20.
That he asked that "the girl" hold it until Nov. 22 for mailing. It
arrived at Somersett's place in time for him to get to Jacksonville
on the 24th and meet Milterr.

Apparently, Milterr flew both ways from Valdosta to Dallas and back.

After they met in Jacksonville, they drove to Columbia, South Carolina,
where they met with a man by the name of Bolton and another man by the
name of Dalton Mimms who owned an electrical shop called Mimms Electrical
Company, 768 Augusta Street, West Columbia. Both of these men are big
shots in the KKK of South Carolina.

This is the first page of a June 5, 1968, memorandum reflecting a conversation between a "Fensterwald" and Bill Somersett. At the time I obtained this copy, the name
Fensterwald was unknown to me. (My note above his name reads, "Who is he?") I
now believe that he was Bernard Fensterwald, a lawyer involved in assassination
research. Page two of this interesting memo is included in the Documents section.   97

The whereabouts of other such named subjects are also included, but obviously Milteer was a principal.

How did an "Agent in Thomasville" verify that Milteer was in Quitman, Georgia, on Nov. 22, 1963, the day of the assassination of President Kennedy?

Was this anonymous "Agent in Thomasville" also the source for info in the FBI Teletype just five hours after the assassination: "Milteer-s whereabouts at Quitman GA., this date ascertained and Secret Service advised," [**Doc.#1**]. Who was this agent?

Royal McGraw had been with me when I received orders from the Atlanta FBI office to go find Milteer minutes after the assassination for the Secret Service. If I had to venture a guess, I would say that officials in the Atlanta office and McGraw in Thomasville controlled the Milteer matter for their own purposes.

I had spent five days, from Nov. 22 to Nov. 27, trying to locate Milteer, and had no idea that there were lies being told about Milteer's whereabouts, effectively taking the pressure off any search or large-scale investigation into Milteer as a suspect.

If the Atlanta FBI office had not said that Milteer was in Quitman, all hell may have broken loose. Since the Secret Service was requesting this determination, that agency, with the assistance of the FBI, should not have stopped until they had located him. I firmly believe that Milteer could have been discovered in Dallas at the time of the killing of the President. This could have caused the investigation to snowball, and all of the information that both agencies had in their hands would have surfaced. That would certainly have changed the course of history!

I can state with certainty that Milteer was not in Georgia on Nov. 22; I was actively looking for him, and he was nowhere to be found until five days later. Then, almost three decades later I read the book *High Treason*, and find a photograph of Milteer looking at the President moments before the shots ring out. Whoa!

With all that was then known, Milteer and his associates should have been held and charged on a conspiracy violation. They might have been, had not documents deflected attention from Milteer, and had Oswald not been arrested and silenced shortly thereafter. Death cemented Oswald's alleged guilt and ended all other investigations.

The June 5, 1968, memorandum referenced earlier [**Doc. #13**], also states that Milteer flew, "from Valdosta to Dallas and back." Was that trip ever checked out? I can find no record that it was.

In addition, in that same memorandum, Somersett explains that Milteer set up an alibi for his trip to Dallas with a letter he wrote to Somersett, which was held by a friend (probably C.C. Cofield) and not postmarked from Georgia until Nov. 22. That letter set up a meeting between Milteer and Somersett at Union Train Station in Jacksonville, Fl., on Nov. 23.

After I had finally located Milteer and brought him in for questioning five days after the assassination, it would have been the perfect opportunity to ask him about the details of what had been said at the October meeting and on the taped Nov. 9th conversation: details about the shooters, the high-powered rifle, the tall-building reference and his whereabouts during the days leading up to, including and then following the assassination.

Of course by the time I had found Milteer, Oswald had been arrested and murdered, but the investigation was ongoing, and I am convinced that Milteer was cocky enough to have made a mistake in a formal interrogation and may have revealed what could have led to further details about the assassination, and possibly even led to those who were in fact behind it.

While the discrepancies between my report and the reports on file are explored in Chapter Eight, there was one glaring inconsistency that surfaced in my research about Milteer, and *that difference has been used to discredit his presence in Dealey Plaza on Nov. 22, 1963.* It's the determination of Milteer's height.

Both Harding's and McGraw's investigative reports state that he was 5'4" tall. The photograph, said to be taken on "11/27/63" by "FBI Agents," has written on its reverse that Milteer's height was 5'5". These statistics have been used by some to disqualify Milteer as being the man in the photograph, because comparison height evaluations of the man in the Dealey Plaza photo have shown him to be taller than 5'4".

I met, detained and stood toe-to-toe with Milteer. Granted, he was shorter than I was (6'7"). However, I know he was taller than 5'4"; in fact, in my descriptive data of Milteer, I wrote that he was 5'8" tall. Years later, due to additional research, my memory of Milteer's height was buttressed by other Secret Service descriptions of Milteer, which lists him as either 5'7" or 5'8".

While the intelligence information about Milteer's threats against the life of the president was made available to the Warren Commission, the final report contains nothing about him, even though there are reams of reference material on Milteer in the National Archives. Missing from the National Archives is my actual investigative FD 302 on Milteer; nor could I find any record of the hate material and some of the other data I had obtained from him during that first background investigation.

Was Milteer a conspirator, or just prophetic, foretelling the assassination of JFK? He was hardly a prophet, but just how involved he really was, we may never know. Like so many others connected to the assassination investigation, Milteer died a mysterious death. In early February of 1974, according to reports, a stove blew up in his house and his legs were badly burned. He was treated in the hospital for two weeks and his burns were healing, but then he suddenly died. Curious. Also curious, the mortician working on his body was reported to have said the damage he saw should not have caused Milteer's death.

Why, with all we suspect about Milteer now, doesn't the government, the Dallas Police Department or a duly empowered panel of experts, using all of the techniques, technology and investigative skills available today, go back to square one and start over? Murder is never a closed case until it is solved.

THE CONFIDENTIAL INFORMANT

William (Willie) Somersett was one of the people connected to the assassination of President John F. Kennedy whose involvement has been played down over the years. Yet it was information provided by Somersett – as a confidential law-enforcement informant – that drew me into the FBI investigation of Joseph Adams Milteer in the weeks before the assassination of the president. I did not know who Somersett was at the time; I discovered it years later when I began looking into the inconsistencies of the investigation. Not only did I discover Somersett's identity, I found evidence that, following the assassination, the FBI began tagging Somersett as a "former unreliable informant."

To review and expand:

William Somersett lived in the Miami area and was known to furnish information to police contacts. In this instance, he knew and cooperated with Lt. Charles H. Sapp of the Intelligence Unit of the Miami, Florida Police Department about a possible assassination attempt on President Kennedy.

William Somersett

Somersett told Sapp that Milteer, and two other persons had a discussion at an Indianapolis, Indiana hotel in the latter part of October 1963, where plans to assassinate President Kennedy were talked about in detail. This was the information I received as a Special Agent for the FBI in a Nov. 13, 1963, phone call from Atlanta SAC Jim McMahon. I was told by McMahon to begin a top-priority investigation based on information received from a reliable informant with both the Miami Police Department and the Miami FBI office. I was to investigate Joseph Adams Milteer and to provide the FBI and the Secret Service with background information on him. That I did, completing my assignment and filing my report on Milteer three days later.

What I did not know at the time was that Somersett had also alerted Sapp that Milteer, his boyhood friend, had come down to Florida for a visit on Nov. 9, 1963, and Lt. Sapp had asked if a police tape recorder could be placed in his apartment so that they could record the conversation between the two of them. Somersett agreed.

On the given date, Milteer and Somersett sat in the apartment and talked about a variety of things. During their discussion, Milteer told his friend that President Kennedy "would be shot from an office building with a high powered rifle." When questioned by Somersett about whether he was serious that they were really going to kill the president, Milteer said, "It was in the works." The entire transcript is currently available on the Internet on several websites, such as www.maryferrell.org. I first saw a partial transcript in Appendix B of *High Treason*.

In the course of my recent investigation, I have found pre-assassination documents from both the Secret Service and the FBI that call Somersett a "trusted confidential informant of ..." and "a source who has furnished reliable information in the past."

Less than a week after the assassination, however, the discrediting of Somersett as a reliable informant began, all while perpetuating the fraud about Milteer's whereabouts:

- A Nov. 27, 1963, FBI Letterhead Memorandum (LHM) [**Doc. #14A**] to Al Belmont (the No. 3 man at the FBI at the time and a confidant of Director Hoover) on the subject of "Assassination of President John F. Kennedy, Nov. 22, 1963, Dallas Texas," references information originally furnished by William Somersett, "a former racial informant," provided in early November about the potential assassination "at some future date." The second paragraph reads in full:

  > It should be noted that Somersett was discontinued as an informant in 1961 for indiscretions on his part which threatened to expose a reliable Bureau informant and that Somersett is regarded as a "professional informant" who is in the business of furnishing information primarily for monetary gains.

- On page two of that Nov. 27 LHM [**Doc. #14B**], there is a sentence that reads: "Atlanta has advised that investigation indicates there is no truth in the information furnished by Somersett and *that Milteer was in Quitman, Georgia on 11/22/63*" [emphasis added]. I was the agent charged with

UNITED STATES GC RNMENT

Memorandum

Doc. #14A

Mr. Belmont

DATE: November 27, 1963

A. Rosen

ASSASSINATION OF PRESIDENT
JOHN F. KENNEDY
NOVEMBER 22, 1963
DALLAS, TEXAS

~~Confidential~~

Information was originally furnished by William
Somersett, a former racial informant, on 11/10/63 to the
effect J. A. Milteer, active in the Constitutional American
Parties of the United States, said plans were being made to
kill the President at some future date and that Jack Brown
could do the job and Milteer would be willing to help. He
added it could be done near the White House with a high-powered
rifle. Jack Brown is the Imperial Wizard of the Dixie Klans,
Knights of the Ku Klux Klan, and he resides in Chattanooga,
Tennessee. This information was immediately furnished to the
Secret Service.

It should be noted that Somersett was discontinued
as an informant in 1961 for indiscretions on his part which
threatened to expose a reliable Bureau informant and that
Somersett is regarded as a "professional informant" who is in
the business of furnishing information primarily for monetary
gains.

Somersett has now advised that he allegedly met Milteer
in Jacksonville 11/23/63. Milteer was described as jubilant over
the President's death and said, "Everything ran true to form.
I guess you thought I was kidding you when I said he would be
killed from a window with a high-powered rifle." Somersett
asked whether Milteer was guessing when he originally indicated
a plan to kill the President and Milteer allegedly replied,
"I don't do any guessing." In a subsequent trip from Jacksonville
to Columbia, South Carolina, Milteer reportedly told Somersett he
had been in Fort Worth and Dallas as well as other southern cities.
He did not indicate the dates of his visits to these cities.

1 - Mr. Mohr
1 - Mr. DeLoach
1 - Mr. Evans
1 - Mr. Sullivan

EX-108   REC-3
230

62-109060-124

25 DEC 2 1963

I didn't find Milteer until after 5 P.M. on Nov. 27, but here is a high-level FBI head office
two-page LHM from Nov. 27, parroting the Atlanta FBI office report that Milteer was in
Quitman. The memo includes some very telling quotes collected from Somersett that
are dismissed as "bordering on the fantastic" (p. 104). Here he is labeled "a 'professional
informant' who is in the business of furnishing information primarily for monetary gains."

Memorandum to Mr. Belmont
RE: ASSASSINATION OF PRESIDENT
    JOHN F. KENNEDY

Milteer also allegedly said he contacted Robert Shelton, Klan leader, Tuscaloosa, Alabama, on the evening before the bombing of the Sixteenth Street Baptist Church in Birmingham. He expressed the opinion Shelton could not be depended upon as Shelton is against violence.

Milteer was further alleged by Somersett to have said that Martin Luther King and Attorney General Kennedy are now unimportant but the next move would be against the "Big Jew." He alleged that at this time there is a communist conspiracy by Jews to overthrow the United States.

On 11/24/63 at Columbia, South Carolina, Milteer indicated to Somersett he may have made a long-distance call and said that they did not have to worry about Oswald getting caught because Oswald knew nothing and the right-wing was in the clear. He added that the "patriots" outsmarted the communists by infiltrating their group in order that the communists would execute the plan without involving the right-wingers. Also at Columbia, South Carolina, Milteer reportedly prepared notes prior to the arrival of members of the Constitutional American Parties of the United States. He captioned his notes "Notice to all Christians" and wrote "The Zionist Jews killed Christ 2,000 years ago and on November 22, 1963, they killed President Kennedy. You Jews killed the President. We are going to kill you." Milteer allegedly signed his notes as "International Underground."

Atlanta has advised that investigation indicates there is no truth in the information furnished by Somersett and that Milteer was in Quitman, Georgia, on 11/22/63. In addition, it has been reliably reported in the past that Jack Brown has furnished deliberately false information to persons he suspects of being informants for the purpose of trapping them if the information is repeated. In connection with the investigation of the Birmingham bombings, Somersett furnished information bordering on the fantastic, which investigation failed to corroborate.

ACTION:
Secret Service is being advised and the Atlanta Office is checking into whether Milteer may have made any long-distance calls during pertinent period, will check out his activities during the pertinent period, and will interview him. Activities of Brown are also being checked during pertinent period.

231

This high-level FBI two-page LHM and the Rowse LHM [Doc. #8] may help us to understand the mechanics of a fraud in which I may have been an unwitting accomplice. According to the Rowse memo, the Washington FBI office contacted the Atlanta FBI office at 2:50 P.M. on Nov. 27th to give me the assignment to interview Milteer: an assignment I had already been given five days earlier. Something was being cooked up.

finding Milteer on Nov. 22, 1963, and he was not found to be in the area around Quitman until five days later.

• On Nov. 29, 1963, an Airtel from the Director to FBI offices in Miami, Atlanta and Knoxville, reads in part, "In view of over-all consideration of information furnished by Somersett to date, much of which is characteristically of a type which cannot be verified or corroborated, and some of which borders on sensational or fantastic, it appears characterization of his reliability as set forth by Miami is not justified. ... It does not appear we are in a position (to) describe all of the information furnished by Somersett in the past as being reliable, and accordingly, the characterization of his reliability should be consistent with this fact."

• The same Airtel goes on to state that "Miami should amend the reliability statement to show that some of the information furnished by Somersett is such that it could not be verified or corroborated. Amended pages should be furnished."

• In that same Airtel there is another interesting sentence: "*Investigation by Atlanta has indicated* there is no truth in the statements by Somersett and *that Milteer was in Quitman, Georgia during the pertinent period.*" [emaphasis added] This is taken almost verbatim from the Nov. 27 memorandum and is not true, for the reasons stated before.

• A three-page FBI Airtel dated Dec. 2, 1963 [**Docs. #15A, 15B & 15C**] contradicts the FBI's attempt to discredit Somersett in the Nov. 29 Airtel. The Dec. 2 Airtel is addressed to the Director, FBI, and is from the Special Agent in Charge, Miami office, and references the threat to kill President Kennedy by J.A. Milteer, Miami, Fla., on Nov. 9, 1963. The Airtel reiterates the Bureau's questioning of Miami's characterization of Somersett as having furnished reliable information in the past. It continues in that vein regarding the Bureau's request that Miami amend its reliability statement about Somersett.

The Miami office (on page 2 of the memorandum) concurs that "much of the information furnished by Somersett is characteristic of the type which could not be verified or corroborated and some of which is bordering on the sensational

F B I

Doc. #15A

Date: December 2, 1963

PLAIN TEXT

Transmit the following in _____

(Type in plain text or code)

Via **AIRMAIL** _____ **AIRTEL**

(Priority or Method of Mailing)

TO   DIRECTOR, FBI ATTENTION: CIVIL RIGHTS SECTION
                           GENERAL INVESTIGATIVE DIVISION

FROM   SAC, MIAMI (157-902) (P)

RE   THREAT TO KILL PRESIDENT KENNEDY
            BY J. A. MILTEER, MIAMI, FLORIDA,
            NOVEMBER 9, 1963,
            (Miami File 157-902)

            ASSASSINATION OF PRESIDENT
            JOHN F. KENNEDY, NOVEMBER 22, 1963,
            DALLAS, TEXAS
            (Miami File 89-35)

        Re Miami airtel and letterhead memorandum dated
11/27/63 and Bureau airtel to Miami dated 11/29/63, with
copies to Atlanta, Knoxville, and Birmingham.

        For the information of Dallas, Denver, and Savannah,
Bureau airtel to Miami dated 11/29/63 questions Miami's
letterhead memorandum characterizing WILLIAM SOMERSETT, as a
source who has furnished reliable information in the past.

        The Bureau has requested Miami to amend the
reliability statement in referenced Miami airtel and letterhead memorandum of 11/27/63. This is being done and the
appropriate number of amended pages are enclosed for the
Bureau and listed offices as set forth below in the copies.

                                                    62-109060

    4 - Bureau (Enc. 8) (AM) (RM)
            (1 - ASSASSINATION OF PRESIDENT JOHN F. KENNEDY
                11/22/63, DALLAS, TEXAS)   NOT RECORDED
    (COPIES CONTINUED PAGE 2)
    4 - Miami (1 - 157-902) (1 - 89-35)   1 DEC 4 1963
            (1 - 157-900) (1 - 137-363 Sub A)

LCP:pp
Approved: _____ Sent _____ M Per _____
5 7 DEC 31 1963   Special Agent in Charge

In this December 2, 1963 three-page Airtel to FBI headquarters, the Miami office writes about being asked to amend their statements that Somersett has furnished reliable information in the past, to unreliable. They acquiesce to a point, but continue their support of their informant (with a little bit of covering their ass) in a very polite manner, "This is being brought to the Bureau's attention since Miami has not knowingly received information from Somersett that would indicate he has furnished false information."

MM 157-902   **Doc. #15B**

Copies Continued:

3 - Atlanta (Enc-3) (AM) (RM)
     (2 - 157- J. A. MILTEER)
     (1 - 157-THREAT TO KILL PRESIDENT KENNEDY)
1 - Birmingham (Info) (RM) (Enc-1)
1 - Knoxville (Info) (Enc-1) (RM)
1 - Denver (Info) (Enc-1) (RM)
4 - Dallas (Enc-4) (AM) (RM)
     (2 - THREAT TO KILL PRESIDENT KENNEDY)
     (2 - ASSASSINATION OF PRESIDENT JOHN F. KENNEDY)
2 - Savannah (Enc-2) (AM) (RM)

          The Miami Office concurs with the Bureau, as noted
in Paragraph 2 of referenced Bureau airtel, that much of the
information furnished by SOMERSETT is characteristic of the
type which could not be verified or corroborated and some of
which is on the sensational or fantastic. In this regard,
reference is made to Miami teletype to the Bureau dated 11/10/63,
captioned "THREAT TO KILL PRESIDENT KENNEDY BY J. A. MILTEER,
MIAMI, FLORIDA, NOVEMBER 9, 1963."

          In this communication, Miami reported information
furnished by SOMERSETT relating to a statement that plans
were in the making to kill President KENNEDY and the job could
be done from an office or hotel in the vicinity of the White
House using a high powered rifle. This information would   *False*
certainly be difficult to verify or corroborate and bears on
sensational or fantastic.

          The Bureau is aware of the conversation between
MILTEER and SOMERSETT that was tape recorded by the Miami
Police Department. The facts as furnished by SOMERSETT to
the Miami Office were consistent with the information in the
recording.

          This is being brought to the Bureau's attention
since Miami has not knowingly received information from
SOMERSETT that would indicate he has furnished false
information.

                              - 2 -

MM 157-902   **Doc. #15C**

          The Bureau and the listed offices are requested
to correct Miami's letterhead memorandum of November 27, 1963,
with the enclosed amended pages.

          They even changed memos
          to protect the Bureau.

or fantastic." The Airtel then references information provided by Somersett and titled "Threat to Kill President Kennedy by J.A. Milteer, Miami, Florida, on Nov. 9, 1963." The Miami SAC agrees that this information would be difficult to verify or corroborate; however, he reminds all receiving this Airtel (including Director Hoover) that:

> The Bureau is aware of the conversation between Milteer and Somersett that was tape recorded by the Miami Police Department. The facts as furnished by Somersett to the Miami Office were consistent with the information in the recording.
>
> This is being brought to the Bureau's attention since Miami has not knowingly received information from Somersett that would indicate he has furnished false information.

• The ambivalence with which the Bureau treated Somersett is evident in a Jan. 22, 1964, FBI document [**Doc. #16**] titled "Joseph Adams Milteer" and written in reference to the report of SA Royal McGraw, dated that same date:

> It says " all sources (except any listed below) ... have furnished reliable information in the past.":
>
> T-2, William Somersett, former Miami 607-C (RAC) is a source who has furnished reliable information in the past and has furnished some information that could not be verified or corroborated.

• Another document [**Doc. #17A & 17B**] I found on the discrediting of Somersett is a Letterhead Memorandum dated Feb. 2, 1967, and it is addressed to Mr. DeLoach at FBI Headquarters from A. Rosen. The memo was sent to advise the FBI that the Miami office had been contacted by Miami News reporter Bill Barry inquiring about a "tape" predicting the assassination of President Kennedy that was made two to three weeks before the event. Under the section headed "BACKGROUND" it states that "He [meaning Barry] was advised the Bureau did not have such a tape and could make no comment about the matter."

The Bureau may not have had a tape, but they and the Secret Service certainly had a record of the tape recording and

Doc. #16

UNITED STATES DEPARTMENT OF JUSTICE

FEDERAL BUREAU OF INVESTIGATION

In Reply, Please Refer to
File No.

Atlanta, Georgia
January 22, 1964

Title   Joseph Adams Milteer

Character

Reference   <u>Report of Special Agent Royal
A. McGraw January 22, 1964, at
Atlanta, Georgia.</u>

       All sources (except any listed below) whose
identities are concealed in referenced communication have
furnished reliable information in the past.

       T-2, WILLIAM SOMERSETT, former Miami 607-C (RAC)
is a source who has furnished reliable information in the
past and has furnished some information that could not be
verified or corroborated.

This document contains neither recommendations nor conclusions
of the FBI. It is the property of the FBI and is loaned to
your agency; it and its contents are not to be distributed
outside your agency.

23

An Atlanta Letterhead Memorandum dated Jan. 22, 1964, referring to Agent
McGraw's report of the same date, shows Somersett's status as an informant is
now one "who has furnished reliable information in the past and has furnished
some information that could not be verified or corroborated." The discrediting
of Somersett continued, and the Atlanta FBI office devalued the allegations of
Milteer's threats in McGraw's report.

Doc. #17A

Tolson
DeLoach
Mohr
Wick
Casper
Callahan
Conrad
Felt
Gale
Rosen
Sullivan
Tavel
Trotter
Tele. Room
Holmes
Gandy

UNITED STATES · GOVERNMENT

Memorandum

TO : Mr. DeLoach

FROM : A. Rosen

SUBJECT: ASSASSINATION OF PRESIDENT
JOHN F. KENNEDY
11/22/63
DALLAS, TEXAS

DATE: February 2, 1967

1 — Mr. DeLoach
1 — Mr. Rosen
1 — Mr. Malley
1 — Mr. Shroder
1 — Mr. Raupach
1 — Mr. Wick

PURPOSE:

To advise the Miami Office has been contacted by a news reporter from the "Miami News" inquiring about a "tape" which was made two or three weeks prior to the assassination of President Kennedy predicting the President's assassination.

BACKGROUND:

Miami advised Bill Barry, news reporter, "Miami News" telephonically contacted the Miami Office and inquired whether the FBI has a "tape" which was made two or three weeks prior to the assassination of President Kennedy predicting President Kennedy's assassination. He was advised the Bureau did not have such a tape and could make no comment regarding the matter. *what about transcript?*

Bureau files reveal that a former racial informant of the Miami Office, William Somersett, was visited by J. A. Milteer of Quitman, Georgia, on 11/9/63. At that time the conversation between Somersett and Milteer was tape recorded by the Miami, Florida, Police Department Intelligence Unit. The recording contained a statement by Milteer in which Milteer advised that plans were in the making to kill President Kennedy at some future date and he indicated the job could be done from an office or hotel in the vicinity of the White House using a high-powered rifle.

The information contained in the tape recording was furnished to U. S. Secret Service by the Miami, Florida, Police Department, date unknown. However, this information was telephonically furnished to U. S. Secret Service Headquarters by the Bureau at 12:15 a.m. 11/11/63. We received Xerox copies of the transcript of the recording and the information regarding the threat to President Kennedy was set forth in a letterhead memorandum furnished to U. S. Secret Service Headquarters through liaison on 11/18/63.

REC- 63   62-109060

ENCLOSURE

KMR:dcs
(7)
Enclosures

2-3-67

CONTINUED — OVER

UNRECORDED COPY FILED IN

This is a Feb. 2, 1967, Letterhead Memorandum (LHM) from Alex Rosen, FBI Assistant Director, to Cartha DeLoach Assistant Director, about an inquiry made at the Miami FBI office by a "Miami news reporter" regarding a tape recording made three weeks prior to the assassination of President John Kennedy predicting the assassination of the president. The reporter was advised that the Bureau (Continued next page→)

Memorandum to Mr. DeLoach
Re: ASSASSINATION OF PRESIDENT JOHN F. KENNEDY

Doc. #17B

Bureau files reveal Joseph Adams Milteer is a 65-year-old wealthy
bachelor, who inherited an estimated $200,000 from his father's estate. He
has been described as an eccentric who has associated with hate-type organizations and formed his own "Constitutional American Parties of the United
States," which is a paper organization having no membership. This information
and complete background regarding Milteer have previously been furnished to
U. S. Secret Service.

William Somersett telephonically contacted the Miami Office on 1/26/67.
He advised he was contacted by Sergeant Everett Kay of the Miami, Florida,
Police Department who requested Somersett's permission to release information
recorded between himself and J. A. Milteer on 11/9/63. Somersett agreed to the
release as long as his identity was concealed. Subsequently, he was contacted
by Bill Barry, reporter for the "Miami News," regarding his conversation with
Milteer. Somersett determined Barry is writing a story for a magazine that
was not identified. Barry feels Secret Service failed to do their job, and the
information furnished to them regarding Milteer confirms his views. According
to Somersett, Barry advised that Robert Kennedy, who was Attorney General
at the time the information from Milteer was received, failed to properly carry
out his duties to help protect the President. Barry noted when President
Kennedy was in Miami prior to his Dallas trip, his security was extremely tight,
and if the same security had been afforded him in Dallas, he would be alive
today. Somersett said Barry made no derogatory remarks concerning the
Bureau but related the story will be critical of Secret Service and Robert Kennedy.

At the conclusion of Somersett's comments, it was forcefully pointed out
to him by the Miami Office the confidential nature of his former association with
the Bureau, and he said he was fully aware of this. Somersett was a criminal
and racial informant who was active from late 1949 until 11/13/61. He has furnished both reliable and unreliable information in the past and was discontinued
because of his unreliability.

It is to be noted that during the investigation of the assassination it was
determined J. A. Milteer was in Quitman, Georgia, on 11/22/63, the date
of the assassination. *[It keeps on going]*

ACTION:

Attached for approval are letters to the Criminal Division of the Department
and the U. S. Secret Service furnishing information concerning this
proposed article.

did not have such a tape and could make no comment. In the very next paragraph
Rosen admitted that such a tape was made on Nov. 9, 1963, by the Miami, Florida
Police Department Intelligence Unit, and on that tape Milteer tells Somersett that
plans were in the making to kill President Kennedy. On page two of the LHM the lie
about Milteer's whereabouts on Nov. 22 continues.

the FBI had "Xerox copies of the transcript of the recording," as is stated later in this memorandum.

•   Also under the heading of "BACKGROUND" in that same 1967 memorandum, the second paragraph mixes up the information from Somersett, through either sloppiness or purposeful obfuscation of the data received. For example, that paragraph discusses Milteer and the plans to kill President Kennedy, saying Milteer "indicated the job could be done from an office or hotel in the vicinity of the White House using a high-powered rifle."

That was the information received from Somersett about the Indianapolis meeting, not what was on the Nov. 9 tape recording.

•   As the memo continues, it states that William Somersett contacted the Miami FBI office to explain that he was contacted by a Sergeant Everett Kay of the Miami Police Department asking to release the information about the Nov. 9, 1963, recording between Somersett and Milteer. Somersett agreed to the release of information as long as his identity was kept secret and he was subsequently contacted by the reporter. Again it is interesting to note that Somersett's association with the FBI is referenced in the following:

> At the conclusion of Somersett's comments, it was forcefully pointed out to him by the Miami Office of the confidential nature of his former associations with the Bureau, and he said he was fully aware of this. Somersett was a criminal and racial informant who was active from late 1949 until 11/13/61. He has furnished both reliable and unreliable information in the past and was discontinued because of his unreliability.
>
> It is to be noted that during the investigation of the assassination, *it was determined J.A. Milteer was in Quitman, Georgia, on 11/22/63, the date of the assassination* [emphasis added].

If Somersett was unreliable, why was the Bureau still accepting information from him in 1963 … information that I investigated about a potential assassination?

Again, as we know, Milteer was *not*, as this memorandum states, in Quitman, Georgia on Nov. 22, 1963. He was in Dallas, Texas, but he was provided an alibi by the FBI. Again, why?

For the FBI to tag Somersett as an "unreliable informant," was to place Somersett in limbo when it comes to his involvement in intelligence circles. The informant literally has no friends; no one trusts him after that word goes out; plus, such a former informant often becomes a target by criminals and many are killed. I always had a problem with this because the information that comes to us from informants cleans up a lot of problems on the street.

Somersett had been an informant for both the Miami Police Department and the FBI for a long time, obviously providing very reliable information that was so recognized in FBI files. Yet, when Somersett's warning about the assassination plots was made public, the wheels went into motion. He was shut down and classified unreliable. Why?

• There is the document found by Kennedy assassination researcher Jeff Caufield of an undated (possibly Feb. 6, 1967) "Memorandum to Mr. DeLoach Re: Assassination of President John Fitzgerald Kennedy." [**Doc. #18**] Keep in mind that Cartha "Deke" DeLoach was very close to FBI Director Hoover and had his ear to everything going on in the Bureau. The first paragraph of that memorandum reads:

> Following the assassination of President Kennedy on 11/22/63, Milteer, because of his known association with hate-type organizations and his previous threat regarding President Kennedy, was immediately considered a suspect. *However, our investigation determined he was in Quitman, Georgia, his home, on 11-22-63* [emphasis added].

• A final document I found on the discrediting of Somersett is a LHM dated March 23, 1967 [**Doc. #19A & 19B**]. Again, the memorandum is addressed to Mr. DeLoach from A. Rosen. This LHM gives the FBI more "cover" as William Somersett is now talking to the press about the Nov. 9, 1963 tape recording, and has written an

ORIGINAL

Doc. #18

J. CAUFIELD

14520 JACKSON ROAD
MORELAND HILLS, OHIO 44022

Memorandum to Mr. DeLoach
RE: ASSASSINATION OF PRESIDENT
JOHN FITZGERALD KENNEDY

~~Following the assassination of President Kennedy on 11-22-63, Milteer, because of his known association with hate-type organizations and his previous threat regarding President Kennedy, was immediately considered a suspect. However, our investigation determined he was in Quitman, Georgia, his home, on 11-22-63.~~

Milteer was interviewed on 11-27-63, which was five days following the assassination of President Kennedy. He was not arrested or detained. At that time he was questioned regarding his travels and association with various organizations. He admitted being a non-dues paying member of the White Citizens Council, the Congress of Freedom, and the Constitutional Party—all right-wing organizations.

In addition, he was questioned concerning whether he ever made any threats to assassinate President Kennedy. At that time, Milteer emphatically denied ever making threats to assassinate President Kennedy or participating in any such assassination.

All information in our possession regarding the threat to President Kennedy and Milteer's activities with various hate-type organizations has been furnished to U. S. Secret Service and to the Department.

Th   -mation concerning the proposed article by Bill Barry was the   of an A. Rosen to Mr. DeLoach memorandum dated 2-2-67, which is attached.

ACTION:

This is submitted for information.

- 2 -

This undated page of a LHM to DeLoach was given to me by J. Caufield, who found it in the course of his research for a book about Milteer. It appears to me that this may be a secondary page from a 2/6/67 memo that is referenced in the Rosen/DeLoach memo of March 23, 1967. The memo above restates misinformation about Milteer's whereabouts, and appears to reference my interview of Milteer on Nov. 27/28, 1963.

114

Doc. #19A

UNITED STATES GOVERNMENT

Memorandum

REC-74

TO : Mr. DeLoach

FROM : A. Rosen

SUBJECT: ASSASSINATION OF PRESIDENT
JOHN FITZGERALD KENNEDY
NOVEMBER 22, 1963
DALLAS, TEXAS

DATE: March 28, 1967

1 - Mr. DeLoach
1 - Mr. Rosen
1 - Mr. Malley
1 - Mr. Shroder
1 - Mr. Raupach
1 - Mr. Sullivan
1 - Mr. Wick

William A. Somersett, Editor and Labor Organizer of the National Federation of Labor (NFL) made available to the Miami Office copies of the "National Federation of Labor News." Somersett prepared this article and carries the caption "Did the Friction Between Robert F. Kennedy and J. Edgar Hoover Cause the Death of President John Fitzgerald Kennedy in Dallas on November 22, 1963?"

In this article Somersett sets forth the question did the Attorney General Robert F. Kennedy help cause the death of his brother by not furnishing more FBI Agents and Secret Service Personnel to protect the President in his trip to Dallas after having been furnished the tape taken by the Miami Police Intelligence Department which stated the assassination of the President was in "the planning?" Somersett also asked the question did Kennedy's disagreement with the Director cause him to refuse the Director's request for more men and protection "in Texas."

Somersett did not expound on his questions. He is attempting to establish there was some correlation between the threat made in Miami concerning President Kennedy and Kennedy's assassination in Dallas. Our investigation clearly established there was no relationship involved. Further, the matter of the protection of the President is strictly under the jurisdiction of the U. S. Secret Service.

The tape recording referred to was that taken by the Miami Police Department on 11/9/63, between William Somersett and J. A. Milteer of Quitman, Georgia. The recording contained a statement by Milteer in which Milteer advised plans were in the making to kill President Kennedy at some future date and that the job could be done from an office or a hotel in the vicinity of the White House using a high-powered rifle. This information was furnished to U. S. Secret Service and the Department by us.

Enclosures

KMR:ctj
(8)

62-109060 - 4934

REC-74 CONTINUED - OVER

18 MAR 31 1967

59 APR 10 1967

Public criticism of the Warren Commission's findings increased in early 1967. as critic Mark Lane was interviewed in *Playboy* magazine's February issue, and on February 17 the *New Orleans States-Item* disclosed New Orleans D.A. Jim Garrison's probe. Also William Somersett began publishing articles about his taped forewarnings of a threat to kill President Kennedy "from an office building with a high powered rifle."

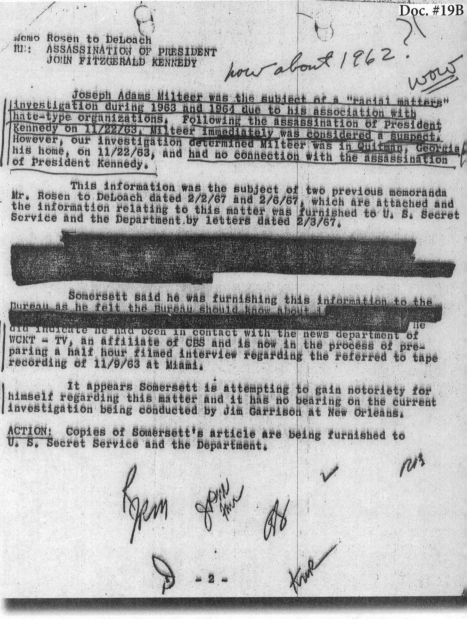

Doc. #19B

Memo Rosen to DeLoach
RE:: ASSASSINATION OF PRESIDENT
JOHN FITZGERALD KENNEDY

how about 1962.   *wow*

Joseph Adams Milteer was the subject of a "racial matters" investigation during 1963 and 1964 due to his association with hate-type organizations. Following the assassination of President Kennedy on 11/22/63, Milteer immediately was considered a suspect. However, our investigation determined Milteer was in Quitman, Georgia, his home, on 11/22/63, and had no connection with the assassination of President Kennedy.

This information was the subject of two previous memoranda Mr. Rosen to DeLoach dated 2/2/67 and 2/6/67, which are attached and the information relating to this matter was furnished to U. S. Secret Service and the Department by letters dated 2/3/67.

Somersett said he was furnishing this information to the Bureau as he felt the Bureau should know about it. He did indicate he had been in contact with the news department of WCKT - TV, an affiliate of CBS and is now in the process of preparing a half hour filmed interview regarding the referred to tape recording of 11/9/63 at Miami.

It appears Somersett is attempting to gain notoriety for himself regarding this matter and it has no bearing on the current investigation being conducted by Jim Garrison at New Orleans.

ACTION: Copies of Somersett's article are being furnished to U. S. Secret Service and the Department.

- 2 -

Here on page two the lie about Milteer's whereabouts on November 22 continues, "… our investigation determined Milteer was in Quitman Georgia, his home on 11/22/63," and a conclusion is presented: "… had no connection with the assassination" I gather this to mean Milteer had no connections to accused assassin Lee Harvey Oswald. Further along in the report the discrediting of the informant continues: "Somersett is attempting to gain notoriety for himself."

article about the Kennedy assassination. On page two of the memo the fraudulent alibi for Milteer's whereabouts continues:

> Joseph Adams Milteer was the subject of a "racial matters" investigation during 1963 and 1964 due to his association with hate-type organizations. Following the assassination of President Kennedy on 11/22/63, Milteer immediately was considered a suspect. *However, our investigation determined Milteer was in Quitman, Georgia, his home, on 11/22/63, and had no connection with the assassination of President Kennedy* [emphasis added].

• And as the memo continues, it gives us another reason for William Somersett's motives:

> It appears Somersett is attempting to gain notoriety for himself regarding this matter and it has no bearing on the current investigation by Jim Garrison at New Orleans.

• Garrison's independent investigation had just recently become public knowledge, when on Feb. 17, 1967, the *New Orleans States-Item* revealed the "JFK Death Plot Probe."

Incredibly, Somersett surfaces again in FBI files and puts himself on the line for others, even after what the Bureau did to him.

On April 3, 1968, Somersett called the Miami Police Department to alert them that he had obtained reliable information that Martin Luther King, Jr. was to be assassinated the next day. Somersett's information was ignored. There is a record of three other calls that day warning of the same thing, also brushed aside.

One day later, on April 4, 1968 Martin Luther King Jr., was assassinated on the balcony of the Lorraine Motel in Memphis, Tennessee.

National Archives and Records Administration

CE 399
FBI C1

National Archives

1985

CHAPTER TEN

A Pristine Bullet?

Single bullet … magic bullet … pristine bullet … the one bullet that supposedly did it all is just another part of the John F. Kennedy assassination story that does not ring true.

It goes beyond the implausible theory of a single bullet, shot from a rifle out of the sixth-floor window of the Texas School Book Depository, entering the back of President's Kennedy's neck, traveling through skin, tissue and bone, causing non-fatal injuries to the President, before exiting at his throat. At that point, this magic bullet makes an abrupt turn in mid-air, travels from the left of Texas Gov. John Connally's back to the right of his back and once again turns left in mid-air before wounding Gov. Connally by entering the right side of his back.

The bullet then exits the governor's chest just under his right nipple, passes though his wrist, enters his thigh, and finally ends up nearly unscathed and pristine when recovered from the governor's stretcher. As improbable as it would be for one bullet to do this kind of damage to two bodies and remain pristine, remember also that at the time of Gov. Connally's surgery in Dallas, bullet fragments were removed from his thigh and even more fragments, as verified by X-rays, remained in Connally's body. In fact, at the time of the governor's death, requests to remove the remaining fragments from Gov. Connally's thigh were refused by Mrs. Connally.

My certainty of the fallacy of the pristine bullet theory goes back to my first days on assignment in Dallas in 1964, when I viewed the Abraham Zapruder film and was taken to that sixth-floor window from which our president was allegedly shot. I say allegedly, because those two experiences led me to doubt that Lee Harvey Oswald

Abe Zapruder (right) describes the President's head wound on television hours after the assassination.

could have been the perpetrator. My doubts were based on two simple facts – President Kennedy's reactions to being shot as recorded for history on the Zapruder film and the improbability of Oswald having the skill to fire three accurate shots from a bolt-action, scoped rifle in 7-1/2 seconds from that window.

The so-called single bullet theory is the main basis on which the Warren Commission findings rely: that Lee Harvey Oswald acted alone and was the sole assassin responsible for the death of President Kennedy and the wounding of Gov. Connally. It is a theory that I do not find to be based on reality.

I have collected books and magazines dating back to the time of the assassination of President John F. Kennedy. Among those, there are several that I would urge readers to examine:

- *Murder in Dealey Plaza,* by Jim Fetzer.

- *Saturday Evening Post* magazine from Dec. 2, 1967, contains photographs of and a comprehensive discussion concerning the pristine bullet.

- *The Killing of a President,* by Robert Groden.

- *Life* magazine from Nov. 25, 1966, and the article "Did Oswald Act Alone? A Matter of Reasonable Doubt."

- *Globe* magazine from Dec. 31, 1991, and the article "Shocking Autopsy Photos Blow Lid off J.F.K. Cover-Up."

- *Vanity Fair* from December 1994, and the article "J.F.K.: Case Reopened."

- *JFK and the Unspeakable,* by James W. Douglas.

- *JFK: Conspiracy of Silence,* by Charles Crenshaw, M.D.

I reference all of the above, because singly, and together they build a case that explodes the myth of the Warren Commission's single-bullet theory and of Oswald being the lone assassin. Some of the above are contradictory, but when taken as a whole they poke holes in the lone assassin theory. Poke enough holes and, usually, nothing is left but a tissue of lies amd misinformation. These references are just the tip of the iceberg of the thousands of writings and exacting, scientific studies conducted over the years. Granted, many of those have been slanted to buttress either anti-conspiracy or pro-conspiracy theories, but at no time has a single commission or agency ever combined all of the reports and evidence to complete a definitive study. Why? If there was a conspiracy to kill the president, has there not been an even more heinous conspiracy since? A conspiracy perpetrated to keep the truth hidden? And after nearly 50 years, isn't it time for the secrecy to be discarded and the truth to be revealed?

I want to briefly outline what I gleaned from the referenced writings and give examples of how these writings influenced my thinking. I do want to preface that with these observations:

- After President Kennedy's killing there was heavy pressure from President Lyndon Baines Johnson to quickly "solve" the case. Once LBJ learned that Lee Harvey Oswald was involved, he saw the opportunity to have Oswald identified as the lone shooter and killer of President Kennedy. After that, everything in the investigation was, in my opinion, slanted to affirm that supposition. Chief among the slanted evidence has to be the many untruths involving the pristine bullet.

- Seconds after shots were fired on that Friday afternoon in Dallas, Lee Harvey Oswald was in the Texas School Book Depository lunch-room drinking a half-finished Coke, where he was confronted by a Dallas police officer. That was at 12:32 P.M. The superintendent of the Book Depository verified that Oswald was an employee, and Oswald was also seen by two other witnesses at that second-floor location around that same time. Oswald was not breathing hard, was not sweating, did not appear excited nor tired from having, if the Warren Commission report is to be believed, shot and killed the president of the United States, hidden the weapon under empty boxes at the opposite side of the building, run the distance from the sixth-floor loft window on the other side of the building and down four flights of stairs to the lunch room, a remarkable feat of self-control and physical conditioning, at the very least.

• There is vast disagreement over the number of shots fired that fateful Friday afternoon, anywhere from three on up to what I believe may have been 11 shots. A number that eliminates Oswald as the "lone" shooter, if he was a shooter at all.

To dispel the pristine-bullet theory, I rely on my years of research on this matter, my 44 years in law enforcement, my eyewitness experiences of gunshot wounds in the Korean War, and a common sense approach.

According to Jim Fetzer's book, *Murder in Dealey Plaza*, a 15-minute telephone conversation took place between LBJ and J. Edgar Hoover at around 9:10 P.M. on the day of the assassination. Several pages later, Fetzer writes, "It is perhaps noteworthy that J. Edgar Hoover has already identified L.H.O. as being the sole assassination suspect (lone nut). There is great reluctance on the part of agents to go against Hoover's assumption. Any leads or revelations to the contrary can now only embarrass the FBI director."

I am convinced that the pristine bullet theory came about because that was the only way Oswald could be identified as the lone assassin. Once Hoover named Oswald as the assassin, very few investigators at a local, state or federal level would or could question that finding. Remember the position of inviolable authority that Hoover had at the time. He and the agency were sacrosanct. Keep in mind also the iron control that Hoover had over "his" agency and the anxiety that permeated the lives and actions of agents who feared the Director's displeasure.

Another section of Fetzer's book deals with Malcolm Perry, M.D., at Parkland Memorial Hospital. Perry was the physician

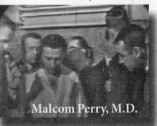

Malcom Perry, M.D.

who performed a tracheotomy on the president once JFK arrived at Trauma Room #1. Perry, along with the other doctors present, observed that, in his experience, the wound to the president's throat resulted from a frontal shot. The tracheotomy itself destroyed any evidence to verify this, but the expertise of the emergency room physicians should have been enough validation for investigators; but that expert observation and medical data did not support the magic bullet theory, and so it was ignored by the Warren Commission.

Evidence was overlooked, witness statements were lost, reports were falsified and the most important criminal investigation this country faced since its creation was tainted, in an effort to paint Oswald as the lone assassin. As a result, the real culprits walked away.

The Dec. 2, 1967 issue of the *Post* magazine and the article titled "Six seconds in Dallas; Major new study shows three assassins killed Kennedy," is a most interesting piece of documentation. That article points to at least three assassins who caught the presidential limousine in a crossfire of four shots: The first, which hit JFK in the back, originated from the Texas Book Depository; the second shot came from a Houston Street building and wounded Gov. Connally. The third shot, also from the Book Depository, hit JFK in the rear of the skull, almost simultaneously with the fourth shot, which was from the front and from the stockade fence behind the grassy knoll, and which struck JFK in the right front of his  head. The force of that shot sprayed blood, bone and brain matter over Jackie Kennedy, the back of the limousine and onto the two motorcycle officers trailing close behind.

There is an excellent diagram accompanying the article that compares the numbered frames in the Abraham Zapruder film (starting with the first shot fired) to a re-enactment and artist's sketch. By comparing the numbered frames of the film and the test results from an FBI firearms expert, the article explains how nearly impossible it would have been for an assassin to have fired the first two shots from the Texas School Book Depository Building.

The article uses the Zapruder film to corroborate eyewitness statements and reports of what happened in Dealey Plaza, including: when shots were first heard, whether that first shot hit the president, and whether a second shot hit Gov. Connally. Interestingly, the article states that, "Not one of the several hundred witnesses that day in Dealey Plaza saw the assassination as the Warren Commission believed it happened ..." and that includes the single bullet that supposedly hit JFK and Gov. Connally.

This is only one of many instances in which eyewitness testimony contradicts the Warren Commission. Even more puzzling is the contradiction between the Warren Commission findings and the testimony of an actual victim – Gov. Connally. The article goes into detail about the Warren Commission's disregard for Connally's recollection of the events. To believe the governor's account – that he was not wounded by the first bullet that hit the president – would mean that there had to have been a at least two assassins.

The evidence clearly disputes these findings. According to the *Post* article, verified by documents in the National Archives, within a week of the assassination, the Secret Service had come to the conclusion that the first and third bullets hit the President and the second bullet, fired by another assassin, hit Gov. Connally.

Additionally, this article goes into great depth regarding the bullet wounds in President Kennedy:

- The entry wound in President Kennedy's upper right back with no exit path to be found, per documentation by an examining doctor. Was this the bullet found on the stretcher in the hospital? The supposition is that during external cardiac massage the bullet worked itself out of the president's body.

- The throat wound defaced by the surgical tracheotomy incision at Parkland Memorial Hospital; the one he so clearly reacts to in the Zapruder film when his arms rise to a horizontal position and his hands close in protectively around his throat.

Essential in dispelling the notion of the pristine bullet, and thus the Warren Commission's findings of Lee Harvey Oswald as the lone assassin, is the number of shots fired and the placement of the shots to President Kennedy's head. The *Post* article also does an exceptional job of detailing this aspect of the assassination based on statements from witnesses, ranging from bystanders to Secret Service agents. For example, the article references S.M. Holland, a signal supervisor for the Union Terminal Railroad, who viewed the events from the vantage point of the railroad overpass; Jean Hill, who was standing near the curb; and Roy Kellerman, a Secret Service agent sitting in the front seat of the limousine. Holland said he heard four shots, and shots three and four were fired in rapid succession; Hill heard more than three shots and said there was a pause between the flurries of shots, which she thought were fired by more than one person; and Kellerman, a trained law enforcement officer, corroborated what Holland said about the last two shots sounding very close together.

S. M. Holland

Jean Hill

Roy Kellerman

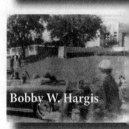
Bobby W. Hargis

In addition to the number of shots fired, the article describes the location of spatter (blood, tissue, bone and brain matter) that went toward the front of the limousine following a shot from behind, as verified by Kellerman and both Connallys, and a greater amount of spatter to the rear left side of the limousine, reaching as far as the motorcycle escorts. In fact, the one officer quoted in the article said, "'It seemed like his head exploded' testified officer Bobby W. Hargis, 'and I was splattered with blood and brain and a kind of bloody water.' The splash of the debris so established in his mind the idea that the shot came from the right front that he got off his cycle and led the chase onto the [Grassy] Knoll."

The *Post* article goes into extensive detail about skull and bone fragments found on Elm Street or the grass just off the street during the afternoon of Nov. 22 and the following day. In those cases, the location where the fragments were found would be consistent only with a shot that originated from the front and right of the motorcade, not from behind. Also, this article includes the detailed testimony of Dr. Robert N. McClelland, who examined President Kennedy at Parkland Memorial Hospital, and McClelland's description of the president's head wound is consistent only with a bullet strike entering from the front and exiting through the rear.

Dr. Robert McClelland: "It was in the right back part of the head – very large ..."

There is much more; but these highlights alone are enough to cast doubt on the pristine bullet theory and by extension the entire Warren Commission report.

Among Robert Groden's numerous books on the Kennedy assassination, *The Killing of a President* goes into extraordinary detail about the number of shots fired that day and the original location of those shots. According to Groden, the second shot fired came from the front and struck the President in the throat, an action substantiated by the Zapruder film. A frontal shot eliminates Oswald as the lone shooter. Groden also writes that the fourth shot struck the President in the back, six inches below the shoulder line and two inches to the right of his spine – corroborated by a photograph of the President's jacket showing a bullet hole in that exact location. Again, the fourth shot takes Oswald out of the picture as the only shooter.

Groden's writings, like an exponential list of other writings, support the contention that the Warren Commission developed the lone gunman and single bullet theory to support their foregone conclusion. This passage in *The Killing of a President* is as succinct as any I have read on debunking the single bullet theory:

> ... one other shot hit the President in the back of the neck, went through his body, exited his throat, continued on to strike Governor Connally by the right armpit, fracturing his fifth rib and collapsing his lung, exiting his chest by the right nipple entering and exiting his right wrist and then burying itself in his left thigh. This undamaged magic bullet later fell off Governor Connally's stretcher at Parkland Hospital. The validity of the single bullet theory dissolves in the face of the hard physical evidence.

In the Nov. 25, 1966 issue of *Life* magazine, there is a story about the assassination titled, "Did Oswald Act Alone? A Matter Of Reasonable Doubt," which explores the question: were President Kennedy and Gov. Connally wounded by the same bullet?

Connally insisted in his testimony to the Warren Commission that he "heard what he instantly identified as a rifle shot. As he was turning to look at the President, he felt a second shot hit him," according to the article. Connally also was able to identify the frames of the Zapruder film in which he was hit: 1.3 seconds after Kennedy reacted. That timing alone is proof of a second assassin, since experts agree that the weapon found on the floor of the Texas School Book Depository Building could not be fired any faster than once every 2.3 seconds.

Another of the publications I have on hand is the *Globe*, dated Dec. 31, 1991, with a front cover story titled "Never Seen Before – Shocking Autopsy Photos Blow Lid Off J.F.K. Cover-Up." Assassination expert Robert Groden is widely quoted in this article, discussing the number of shots fired from high-caliber weapons at the motorcade. According to the article, Groden states that the first shot missed, the second shot hit the President in the throat, and the "fifth shot caused the mortal head wound." That shot was fired

from in front of the limousine by someone on the Grassy Knoll.

What is even more interesting in this article is the reported "disappearance" of two bullet wounds. Accompanying the article is what is identified as an autopsy photo of JFK's body that clearly shows two bullet holes in his back, both located to the right of the spinal column and about 5 or 6 inches below his right shoulder. Adjacent to that photo is what is identified as a government drawing showing a neck wound and no bullet holes in the President's back. And it is that "drawn" neck wound that, per the Warren Commission Report, was the entrance site for the single bullet and around which the entire lone assassin theory was concocted.

The December 1994 issue of *Vanity Fair* includes an article titled "J.F.K.: Case Reopened," authored by Anthony and Robbyn Summers. Interestingly, the article explains that shortly after the assassination, a slight majority of the American public believed the assassination had been a conspiracy. Thirty years later, a news poll reported that 89 percent of the public then believed in a conspiracy and 81 percent of the public were convinced that there had been an official cover-up of the assassination.

A number of observations in this article are worth listing here, including the fact that Kenneth O'Donnell, President Kennedy's close friend and assistant, reportedly said he had been pressured by FBI Director J. Edgar Hoover to "not say what he firmly believed, that gunfire had come from in front of the motorcade." Here is yet another witness to shots coming from somewhere other than the Texas School Book Depository.

The article goes on to state that Senator Richard Schweiker, who spearheaded the Intelligence committee probe, believed "the Warren Commission was set up at that time to feed pabulum to the American people for reasons not yet known, and that one of the biggest cover-ups in the history of our country occurred at that time."

Also included in this piece are details about the recorded phone conversations dealing with the formation of the Warren Commission, which President Lyndon Johnson formulated; how that commission would merely "rubber-stamp" a report that FBI Director Hoover would provide; that the American public needed to be convinced that Oswald was the lone assassin; that Texas law required an autopsy be performed on the President's body, but the Secret Service would not allow that to happen; that none of the doctors performing the autopsy on the President's body at Bethesda Naval Hospital was a practicing forensic pathologist; and an autopsy sketch, the death certificate, a report by FBI agents present at the autopsy, the statements of several Secret Service agents, and the holes in Kennedy's jacket and shirt differ from the Warren Commission report.

There are further inconsistencies with respect to the number of bullet fragments recovered, according to this article. Nurse Audrey Balogh stated that she saw and handled four or five bullet fragments, and that the "smallest was as big as the striking end of a match, the largest twice that size." She said she had seen a picture of the pristine bullet, and questioned how it could have been the bullet from which the fragments came.

JFK and the Unspeakable: Why He Died & Why It Matters by James W. Douglas, was published in 2008 and is an exhaustive work that explores the years of John F. Kennedy's presidency. Douglas' premise is based on the contention that the years during which Kennedy served as president transformed him, essentially, from a warrior to a peacemaker, willing to take the United States out of the hands of the military-industrial-intelligence establishment and create, as Douglas says, a "vision of peace." That transformation, according to Douglas, was the reason the president had to be eliminated.

Most relevant in Douglas' writing from my perspective is the multitude of inconsistencies surrounding the investigation of the assassination. Douglas tracked down and talked to many people who were present that day in Dealey Plaza. He compiled witness accounts of the happenings that day in Dallas that were purposefully excluded from the Warren Commission report, including a number of witnesses who talked to or were confronted by men who identified themselves as Secret Service agents when, in fact, there were no Secret service agents not directly around the presidential motorcade. So who were these men? He details an examination of the fraudulent, but "official," X-rays of JFK's skull that were in total opposition to eyewitness statements from medical professionals at Parkland Memorial Hospital. So how did the president's skull wounds change so drastically from the hospital trauma room to the Bethesda Naval Hospital autopsy site?

Douglas also points out the extraordinary number of violent deaths that can be traced directly back to the assassination of the president and the subsequent investigation, and, in an ironic twist of fate, Joseph Adams Milteer, the man I investigated, just happens to be one of those deaths. Although there are many other inconsistencies that Douglas discovers, I do want to highlight the meticulous examination he does of the life of Lee Harvey Oswald and the still unanswered questions concerning the role Oswald played in this tragedy. Douglas builds a credible case for the deception and plot orchestrated to frame Oswald as the scapegoat in the assassination, from his travels to Russia, his subversive activities in New Orleans, to his relationship with Jack Ruby. Of particular importance in this chapter is Douglas's research concerning the whereabouts of Oswald when the assassination took place; which corroborate, once again, my contention that Oswald could not have been the lone assassin vilified in the Warren Commission report.

Douglas's book is one of the more recent publications on the assassination/conspiracy, and he utilizes the benefit of historical perspective, as well as sources and documents only obtainable in the past few years.

The final publication that I want to reference here is *JFK: Conspiracy of Silence*, by Charles Crenshaw, M.D. Dr. Crenshaw was one of the surgeons who worked on President Kennedy in Trauma Room One at Parkland Memorial Hospital. Two days later, Dr. Crenshaw operated on Lee Harvey Oswald, after he was gunned down in the Dallas Police Department basement. It was 29 years after the events of that fateful weekend that Dr. Crenshaw went public with his observations. His book details

Dr. Charles Crenshaw: "The wound was the size of a baseball."

his reasons for keeping silent for all that time and his fear of what going public with his knowledge would mean:

> Through the years, there have been a thousand instances when I have wanted to shout to the world that the wounds to Kennedy's head and throat that I examined were caused by bullets that struck him from the front, not the back, as the public had been led to believe. Instinctively, I have reached for the telephone many times to call a television station to set the story straight when I heard someone confidently claim that Oswald was the lone gunman from the sixth floor of the Texas School Book Depository, only to restrain myself – until now.

Additionally, Dr. Crenshaw writes about a call he says he received from LBJ while operating on Oswald requesting that the doctor get a deathbed confession from his patient, a request which Dr. Crenshaw says in his book defies logic.

It is Dr. Crenshaw's contention that neither Lyndon B. Johnson nor J. Edgar Hoover was knowledgeable about and/or part of any conspiracy to kill President Kennedy. Nonetheless, I believe both became willing accessories after the fact. Johnson and Hoover were close friends, and both felt threatened by the young president. Johnson was fearful that Kennedy would drop him as a running mate and his vice presidential candidate in the 1964 presidential election. Hoover expected Kennedy to force him to retire as Director of the FBI if Kennedy was re-elected.

Johnson, fearing a conspiracy in the death of President Kennedy, had to know that a lone assassin, AKA Lee Harvey Oswald, was a politically expedient sacrificial lamb to quash any talk of conspiracy. Hoover had to know that if he could manipulate the evidence, easily done given his iconic stature as Director of the FBI, he could be certain that the Warren Commission would have no recourse other than to name Oswald the lone assassin. I am convinced that is exactly what happened with this investigation.

Dr. Crenshaw's writings irrefutably contradict the Warren Commission findings, most particularly with respect to how

President Kennedy was mortally wounded, but additionally with regard to the conspiracy to name Oswald as the lone assassin. If one lie, one untruth is contained in the Warren Commission Report, many more lies are present. That makes the entire Warren Commission report a fraud.

Chapter Eleven

Players and Patsies

Hundreds, if not thousands, of people – investigators, politicians, witnesses, government officials, suspects, and medical experts, can be linked to the assassination of President John F. Kennedy. Scores of books and articles have been written detailing their respective involvement in this unsolved, criminal act. Others, far more knowledgeable than I, have conducted extensive research and evaluations of the relevant roles of the people involved. Nonetheless, I have some personal insights about some of the players I would like to share.

Lyndon Baines Johnson

As a young Texan wanting to get started in politics, LBJ gave up his principles and cheated to win nomination and election to the U.S. Senate, according to fellow Texan, rancher, political activist and historian J. Evetts Haley. The story of how LBJ accomplished this is in a book by Haley titled, *A Texan Looks at Lyndon: A Study in Illegitimate Power*.

If what Haley writes is accurate (and numerous other books and articles tell much the same story), then LBJ's foundation for his career in public service was dishonest from the beginning. Once he started down that road, LBJ never looked back. He was as ambitious as he was politically astute; a master manipulator in getting what he wanted because he made it a point to know as much as he could about his friends and foes alike. Also, LBJ had friends in high places like Sam Rayburn, Speaker of the House of Representatives for an unprecedented 17 years.

The legislative career of LBJ began after his election as U.S. representative for Texas' 10th Congressional District, which he held from 1937 to 1949. He ran for the U.S., Senate in 1949, a disputed election in which instances of fraud were alleged by both candidates and their respective supporters. LBJ eventually won the Democratic nomination and spent the next twelve years in the U.S. Senate, six years as Majority Leader, two years as Senate Minority Leader and two as Senate Majority Whip. In those years, LBJ became one of the most effective and powerful senators in

history. But his ultimate goal was to become President of the United States.

In the presidential election of 1960, Sen. John Fitzgerald Kennedy became the Democratic standard bearer and the eventual party nominee against Vice President Richard Nixon. Knowing that the ticket would need the support of the Southern Democrats, Kennedy was reluctantly convinced to offer the vice-presidency to LBJ.

That role left LBJ with far less power than he had in the U.S. Senate and virtually no influence in the Kennedy White House. LBJ strongly disliked John Kennedy, and the feeling was mutual. Each time they were together, the association grew more antagonistic. Add to that less-than-amicable relationship the damaging publicity from the Bobby Baker scandal in 1963 involving allegations of bribery, financial malfeasance and influence peddling on the part of Baker, an LBJ protégé and friend. Johnson began to realize there was the possibility that President Kennedy would

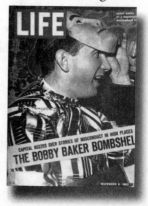

dump him and select another vice-presidential candidate in the 1964 election.

LBJ developed a close friendship with J. Edgar Hoover. The two of them lived across the street from each other  and had meals together frequently. Hoover hated the Kennedys: both the president, whom he feared would force him to retire, and the president's brother Robert, who as Attorney General was Hoover's immediate boss. Johnson and Hoover, powerful in their own right and very knowledgeable about how to play the political game, were allies through resentment and hatred.

There is even talk with some tantalizing evidence that Johnson may have blackmailed Kennedy and his advisors into naming LBJ as the vice-presidential candidate using information supplied by Hoover about certain untold sexual escapades touching national security, and Kennedy's personal health issues. According to several accounts Stuart Symington, a four-term Senator from Missouri, had gone to bed secure that the VP nomination was his, only to wake up in the morning to find that he had been dumped for Johnson.

The 1963 trip to Texas, LBJ's home state, in late November, was to assuage the influential Texas Democrats and to ensure that their support could be counted on in the upcoming election. LBJ was included in this trip and, in fact, rode two cars behind the presidential motorcade along the Dallas streets that Friday afternoon.

Madeleine Duncan Brown, a former mistress of LBJ, describes in her book, *Texas in the Morning*, how less than two months after the assassination, Brown was with LBJ and she asked him about the rumors circulating in parts of Texas about his involvement with the assassination. His

Madeleine Brown

angry response, according to her book, was that the president had to be "taken out," and that the assassination was a decision reached by the CIA and the oil men.

After Kennedy was assassinated, LBJ allegedly told Hoover that Oswald was the assassin, and Hoover sent out that message. From that moment on, all of the work on the investigation conducted by the FBI and passed down to the Dallas Police Department, other police agencies and even to the Warren Commission was channeled toward building a case that portrayed Oswald as the lone assassin. To accomplish this, distortions, the twisting of facts, changing of investigations, evidence lost or destroyed, witness statements discounted, etc. were used over and over again.

President Kennedy was killed by sinister forces in a conspiracy that has yet to be solved. Oswald was, as he said to a reporter while walking down the hallway of the Dallas Police Department, "a patsy."

When someone of importance is assassinated, the first question asked should be: *Cui Bono?* – "Who gains from this?"

In this case, Lyndon Baines Johnson was one of those gaining the most: he became President of the United States. He may not or may have been *the* ringleader, as many assert, but at the very least, he would have to be on board for any cover-up to survive.

J. EDGAR HOOVER, DIRECTOR, FBI

If one looks clearly at the entire window concerning the assassination and asks what one major player could influence the investigation, the answer would have to be J. Edgar Hoover.

I do not make that powerful statement lightly. Nonetheless, I have come to believe that it was the actions of the director of the FBI that facilitated the cover-up.

Hoover was the first director of the Federal Bureau of Investigation and served in that capacity for 48 years, from 1924 to 1972, when he died. During those years, Hoover built the FBI into the country's preeminent crime-fighting agency.

The day I entered on duty as a Special Agent for the FBI was the proudest day of my life. I was proud because I was joining what, in my opinion, is the greatest law enforcement agency in the world. It goes without saying that the FBI became what it is because of Hoover. He laid the solid foundation that remains to this very day.

Whenever I had the chance during the time I was in training in Washington, D.C., I would go to the FBI parking area where Hoover's car was parked. I would time my arrival to coincide with Hoover's and watch as he walked up the few steps and then got into the elevator. There were even times when I shared the elevator with him. I never said a word; I admired him so much that it was enough to be near him. As a new agent, I felt that I was quietly saying thanks.

I was filled with deep pride to have the opportunity to be an agent. Coming from the small town of Barberton, Ohio, I truly believed I was blessed to have been chosen for the FBI, and I had the highest respect for Hoover ... then.

When he was appointed as the new Director of the nascent Bureau of Investigation, Hoover was a young man known for his high standards and principles. As the years passed, he became one of the most powerful men in this country. Unfortunately, I believe, he reached a point where he felt he could do no wrong.

He blinded himself to the principles and values on which he built the Bureau. J. Edgar Hoover let power, recognition, perfection in the public's eye, and ideological friendships close his eyes and change those principles drastically.

Hoover's power came from the agency's vast informational resources, which provided him with information about people in all walks of life. Hoover received, without question, the FBI budget appropriations every year from Congress. He ran the agency with an iron fist, and there was never a question of who was in charge. The FBI was his life, and he always knew what was going on, down to the smallest detail.

For all his dedication to law enforcement and rooting out criminal activity, Hoover had his weaknesses, not the least of which was blinding himself to organized crime's involvement in various activities, including horse racing, for which Hoover had a proclivity. In fact, not until John and Bobby Kennedy were in office did any real push against the "mob" begin; and that push came from the Attorney General, not the director of the FBI. Taking orders was not Hoover's style and he may have begun to sense that he had met his match in the Kennedy brothers, who were not afraid of the power he wielded.

Hoover, at the least, would had to have been party to any cover-up.

ROBERT GEMBERLING

Robert Gemberling is a name that the average person would not recognize; however, his name and the work he did on the post-assassination investigation is an essential part of any analysis of the crime.

Gemberling is a former Special Agent of the FBI, now deceased. He was a street agent working in the Dallas FBI Office during the time of the JFK assassination. Dallas Special Agent in Charge J. Gordon Shanklin appointed Gemberling to coordinate the assassination and Oswald investigations, and as Supervisory Special Agent, he worked on the

investigation until his retirement in December of 1976. Among his duties, Gemberling prepared the 800-plus page report that was the foundation of the Warren Commission's verdict.

I knew Gemberling as a casual friend when we worked together in Dallas. I liked him, and he appeared to be a very friendly person. What I didn't like was the information he put into his report which became the official word of the United States government – that Lee Harvey Oswald was the lone assassin.

Long after we had both retired, Gemberling read a newspaper article sent to him by a mutual friend of ours. It was an interview I had given to a reporter at the *Akron Beacon Journal*, which was published on Sunday, Nov. 22, 1998. In that article, I went on record against the lone gunman theory. Gemberling contacted me by letter the following January and wrote that he was very "disturbed" by what I had told the reporter. Then he spent the remainder of the two-and-a-half page letter alternately attempting to disprove my contentions and criticizing me. I responded to him in an 11-page letter some months later, dissecting his letter, line by line, and answering all of his concerns. When he wrote back, he demeaned my writings and my "ridiculous theories."

Gemberling gave an interview in December 1997 to the *Grapevine*, which is the publication for retired FBI agents. In that article, he was critical of the movie *JFK*, its producer Oliver Stone, and those who believed that a conspiracy existed. He wrote, among other things, about Oswald being the lone shooter; how Oswald had been observed in the loft window of the Texas School Book Depository; how Oswald fired three rounds in seven-and-a-half seconds from a bolt-action, scoped rifle; and that the shots hit President Kennedy from above and behind in the back of his head. This was simply reiteration of what he had written soon after the assassination more than thirty years before.

After that first article and the subsequent correspondence between the two of us, Gemberling prepared another two-page article for the *Grapevine*, published in November 2003, reinforcing the same beliefs that he had written about six years earlier. This was a total antithesis to what my research was showing: that President Kennedy was hit in his throat with a round from the front and in his right temple with another round from the front that blew out the back of his head. Once I read Gemberling's second article, I knew that nothing would change his beliefs, not even evidence that should have at least made him question the veracity of his investigation.

I have come to believe that Gemberling could not be dissuaded because he was following LBJ and FBI Director Hoover's directive that Oswald had to be the shooter. Gemberling wrote of the outstanding work done by the FBI agents in this investigation and how proud he was of their work. But that work was tainted by corruption from above. Whether they knew for certain or merely had suspicions as to the truth, they had to follow the direction given to them. There are too many witness statements from too many different people that contradict the official findings.

On Dec. 21, 2003, I sent all of the writings between Gemberling and me to Don Witham, Editor of the *Grapevine*, in Quantico, VA. I asked him to review the information and then provide authorization for me to write an article to counter what Gemberling had written twice. I explained that I wanted to offer the facts and evidence I had so that retired FBI agents could read another side of the case and draw their own conclusions. I did not receive a reply. I wrote to him again, on Feb. 17, 2004, and this time he did respond, saying he had received all of the material and that it had been reviewed by the staff, including Scott Erskine, executive director of the Retired Agents Association, and several others. The decision was made to not publish any of my work because they did not want to create a confrontational situation between two agents on material each had submitted.

I knew before I sent the material what their decision would be, but I had to try. In no way could they permit me to challenge all that had been written by the FBI and in more than 2,000 publications nationwide. They had to shut me down, at least in that venue, and they did; but not forever.

LEE HARVEY OSWALD

Lee Harvey Oswald has become entwined with "infamous" assassins through history: John Wilkes Booth, James Earl Ray, Sirhan Sirhan, and Mark David Chapman in the United States, alone. It is my belief that Oswald does not merit that notoriety, and that he was the scapegoat for the murder of the president.

How well I remember seeing Oswald on television late on Nov. 22, 1963. He was being escorted down the hallway in the Dallas Police Department and replied to a reporter's question by saying, "I'm just a patsy." I believe he was set up long before the assassination took place.

Part of the conversation recorded on Nov. 9, 1963 between police informant William Somersett and Joseph Adams Milteer explains the role Oswald unknowingly ended up playing.

> *Somersett:* Boy, if that Kennedy gets shot, we have got to know where we are at. Because you know that will be a real shake–
> *Milteer:* They wouldn't leave any stone unturned there. No way. They will pick up somebody within hours afterwards ... just to throw the public off.
> *Somersett:* Oh, somebody is going to go to jail if he gets killed.
> *Milteer:* Just like Bruno Hauptmann in the Lindbergh case you know.

Many researchers have written volumes on Oswald. One of the most comprehensive and most recent is the analysis I found in James W. Douglas' *JFK and the Unspeakable*, a masterful job in tracking down witnesses, tracing the steps of Oswald before, during and after the assassination; compiling evidence of a conspiracy, complete with Oswald look-alikes, and detailing a timeline that makes Oswald's involvement in both the Kennedy assassination and the cold-blooded killing of Dallas Police Officer J.D. Tippit an impossibility.

I do not believe that Oswald fired a single shot at President Kennedy. It is my opinion that Oswald worked for the U.S. government for several years and that he continued in that capacity up until his murder by Jack Ruby on Nov. 24, 1963. I base that opinion on the three-and-a-half years I spent in the U.S. Army and my 20 years in the FBI. Those years give me a depth of understanding about how government service works.

I've referenced *High Treason*, by Robert J. Groden and Harrison E. Livingstone on a number of occasions. On page six in the Introduction, the authors have this to say about Oswald:

> He became fluent in Russian while a U. S. Marine, and it is not credible that he would be stationed at the CIA base at Atsugi, Japan (the base from which U-2 flights were flown over the Soviet Union) as an admitted "Marxist" speaking fluent Russian without being a trusted Agent. Many facts make it clear that his much publicized defection to the Soviet Union was staged. He was probably sent to the Soviet Union by the Office of Naval Intelligence or the CIA, and then repatriated.

After reading this, along with a number of other sources that document the same scenario, how can one not suspect that Oswald's movements and activities were sanctioned by U.S. government officials? Here is Oswald, a Marine radar operator with an above top-secret clearance at a location from which the CIA's U-2 spy planes flew. Then Oswald is assigned to a Marine Corps base in California, from which he continues to work as a

Lee & Marina leaving Minsk, 1962

radar operator, privy to an extraordinary range of military information. Yet two months after his discharge from the Marines, in late 1959, Oswald is in Moscow at the American Embassy declaring his intention to defect to the Soviet Union and making no secret of the fact that he had military secrets he would divulge to the

Soviets. He "defects" to the Soviet Union, works at a factory in Minsk, meets and marries Marina and they, together, return to the United States in mid-1962.

It is impossible to believe that the anti-American statements and actions attributed to Oswald would have been so cavalierly dismissed by the U.S. government, let alone be immune to prosecution for treason, had he not been connected to the intelligence community: the CIA and/or the FBI.

Much has been written about Oswald being a malcontent and bouncing around from location to location after he and Marina settled back in this country. There is evidence of his being interviewed in various locations by FBI agents during these years when he was continuing to present himself as pro-Communist and pro-Castro; yet there are also accounts of his being anti-Communist and anti-Castro. One of Oswald's most interesting and well-documented relationships during this time was the one he had with Guy Banister.

Banister was a former FBI agent, with a storied career that included the killing of John Dillinger. He was one of J. Edgar Hoover's star agents, a law-and-order aficionado who eventually headed up the agency's Chicago office before retiring from the FBI to become the deputy chief of police in New Orleans. Known to have worked closely with the CIA and the Office of Naval Intelligence his whole career, Banister hooked up with Oswald in New Orleans in 1963. Oswald's offices for the Fair

Guy Banister

Play for Cuba Committee were in the same building that housed Banister's office. They allegedly were friends and met in those offices, sometimes daily. What would such a rigid law and order man like Banister have in common with a former Soviet defector like Oswald? The supposition has been that Oswald was acting as an intelligence agent for Banister.

One final irony of that relationship has to be the death of Banister and his business partner Hugh Ward, both of whom died suspiciously within a few days of the Warren Commission's completion of its hearings. Ward died when a plane he was piloting crashed in Mexico. Banister reportedly died of a heart attack, although there are those who say he had a bullet hole in his body.

Another major aspect of Oswald's involvement in the assassination of the president was the happenstance of Oswald having secured a job in the Texas Book Depository just five weeks prior to the assassination – a job he took even though the following day he was called about a better paying and more stable position at Trans Texas Airways. This placed him right where he needed to be and was no mere coincidence. We know that a lot of early planning had to have gone into arranging the logistics of the assassination – the placing of the shooters so strategically that all were able to get off their shots and melt away without being detected or ever identified –and the set-up of Oswald as a "patsy." He had to be targeted as a key person in that planning very early on.

Part of that targeting has to be the threatening letter that Oswald, if it was Oswald, supposedly left at the Dallas FBI office two weeks before the assassination. In Chapter Seven, I wrote about how I learned of the threatening letter twelve years after the assassination. This was the letter that Oswald supposedly threw on the desk of Nan Fenner, asking her to get it to Special Agent James Hosty. The letter warned Hosty not to talk again with Oswald's wife or he would "blow up the Dallas Police Department or the FBI office," with the latter words visible and remembered by Fenner in her testimony later.

Why, with the president due in town in the next two weeks, did the FBI not alert the Secret Service? Why, with this threat, was Oswald not put under surveillance before and during JFK's time in Dallas? Why was the letter itself destroyed just hours after Oswald's death in an apparent conspiracy including Hosty, FBI Special Agent in Charge J. Gordon Shanklin and maybe even FBI

Director J. Edgar Hoover? Why was the existence of the letter not reported as critical evidence to the Warren Commission? Why, after the existence of the letter was uncovered in 1975, was there no detailed investigation regarding it, especially the testimony of Shanklin, who insisted under oath that he did not order the note destroyed? If he did not order the note destroyed, who did?

One reason behind this could be that there was already an assassination plot in the works, and Oswald's role as the "lone gunman" had to be preserved. If the note had gone through proper channels it would then have jeopardized a plot to kill the president. Those planning the assassination could not allow that to happen.

There are many more inconsistencies, false trails of evidence, a series of impersonators, and numerous cover-ups with respect to Oswald that have been discovered in the years since the assassination, far more than I can enumerate here, including Oswald's admiration and respect for JFK, according to evidence supplied by his wife, Marina. However, one additional factor deserves mentioning – the "Babushka Lady."

Beverly Oliver is alleged to be the "Babushka Lady," a witness to the assassination who took a close-up 8mm film of the killing of President Kennedy. Her presence was documented in the Abraham Zapruder film, but her identity was not known until some 10 years later. Oliver was 19 years old at the time of the assassination, and she was reportedly a stripper at a  club next door to Jack Ruby's Carousel Club in Dallas. Oliver confirms that she filmed the death of the president, but states that she never saw the film itself. According to her, the film was

Beverly Oliver: "The whole back of his head went flying out the back of the car."

seized by an FBI Agent whom she identified later as Regis Kennedy, and it was never returned to her. What happened to that film is a question that has never been answered.

Oliver is also important because she corroborates ties between Oswald and Jack

Ruby. That corroboration strengthens the contention of Robert Oswald, Lee's brother, and other patrons of the Carousel Club, that Lee and Ruby knew each other. Oswald was also in contact with others who were directly or indirectly involved in President Kennedy's assassination.

Improbable as it may seem, Oliver has stated that Ruby introduced Oswald to her as "Lee Oswald from the CIA." Oliver also stated that she remembered seeing Oswald with Ruby in a meeting at the Carousel Club one week before the assassination. Also at that meeting were a number of other people, including Charles Harrelson and Jerry Ray James, among others. Harrelson is discussed later in this chapter, as part of the section titled "Three Tramps." James became known to me when I worked in the FBI

Beverly Oliver, 1960s

resident agencies of Dallas and Lubbock, Texas. He headed up a gang of thieves, bank robbers, drug peddlers, prostitutes and pimps. He fancied himself to be a latter-day Al Capone, at least until he was captured, tried and jailed – one of the criminals I most enjoyed "putting away." For Oswald to be in the company of criminals like that tells me that he truly was a "patsy," and/or possibly under cover working to infiltrate the conspiracy. There is Oswald, in the presence of the man who eventually kills him before he has the chance to tell anyone the details of what he knew. Having become aware of the assassination plans, Oswald had to possess a lot of information that could have helped to solve the killing of the president. He couldn't be left alive with that kind of knowledge, and Jack Ruby made sure he wasn't.

JACK RUBY

Jack Ruby played at being the little guy who owned a nightclub who wasn't really involved with anyone. But if you were alive in 1963, the name Jack Ruby is a name you will always remember.

Ruby and Lee Harvey Oswald were linked in November of 1963 and will never be separated.

Millions of people were watching television on Sunday morning, Nov. 24, 1963, as the events following President John F. Kennedy's assassination unfolded. They saw a handcuffed Oswald being moved through the basement of the Dallas Police Department to be transported to the jail at the Sheriff's Office. Then they watched in disbelief as Ruby, who was among a mix of police officers, members of the news media and others,

lunged out of the crowd toward Oswald. There was a pop as Ruby shot Oswald point blank in the stomach. Oswald died hours later in Trauma Room Two at Parkland Memorial Hospital, the same hospital where two days before President John F. Kennedy was pronounced dead.

When arrested, Ruby stated that he killed Oswald because he was so distraught after the assassination of the president he loved – another of the many stories that were perpetrated to camouflage the truth behind the killing of JFK.

Who was Ruby and what made him tick?

Jack Rubenstein was born in 1911 to Joseph and Fanny Rubenstein, who lived in a poor Jewish neighborhood in Chicago. His family moved around a lot, mostly to apartments in poorer ethnic neighborhoods, mostly Italian, where crime was an everyday occurrence.

Ruby's biographical information shows he was a problem child; he had trouble in school and at age 11 was referred for psychiatric treatment. He eventually ended up being placed in a foster home, with little positive effect. In his youth, he allegedly became a "runner" for the Al Capone gang, where he and his gang friends were paid to "run errands."

Ruby left school for good when he was 16, and found a job with Local No. 20467, a junk and scrap dealers' union in Chicago. Eventually working his way up to a leadership role in the union, Ruby fostered and developed even more ties to the mob. In the late 1930s, the State of Illinois seized and audited the books of the union, and determined it to be a "shakedown operation" involved with the mob. During this time, the man who founded the union and supposedly gave Ruby his job, Leon Cooke, was shot and killed.

Paul Dorfman, who was well known in underworld circles and as the trade union liaison man of the Chicago unions, took over Local No. 20467 as its new leader, and Ruby was moved to a position as the second man in charge. He remained active with the union until getting involved with Chicago "strip joints," which had been mob-controlled for decades. This became his main interest, and he later managed some very reputable strip joints, information which the Warren Commission later used to emphasize Ruby's ties to the "underworld."

Ruby spent almost three years in the armed services during World War II until his discharge in early 1946. Around this time, he started traveling to New Orleans with an associate, Hershey Colvin, which is how Ruby's ties to the South began.

In 1947, the mob decided that Dallas might be a good location to set up operations. The city, and in fact the entire state, was wide open. Reportedly some 25 "thugs" from Chicago, including Ruby, went to Dallas to establish those operations.

In conversations with his new friends, Ruby frequently told them he was sent to Dallas by "them." Every time Ruby talked

about past contacts from Chicago, he always referred to those contacts as "them," being very careful to not name names. Once in Dallas, Ruby was involved in several failed strip clubs, and was arrested but not charged by the narcotics bureau of the Dallas Sheriff's Department. He eventually ended up as joint owner of the Carousel Club with partner Ralph Paul.

Ruby's underworld career added three new interests in Dallas – illegal gambling, narcotics and prostitution, which led him deeper into organized crime and connections with the "Mafia."

In fact, there are even indications that Ruby's activities involved gun smuggling to Cuba. This is where he supposedly became known to the CIA, which turned a blind eye to the illegal shipments of arms to that island country in the midst of a revolution. Thus, a tie was formed between the country's intelligence community and a known low-level criminal.

The Dallas Police Department built a file on Ruby's activities, but Ruby was smart. He passed out bottles of liquor and other favors to the police officers; he reportedly let the officers use his room for their "friendships" with the strippers; and he made his women available to the officers. By opening his clubs to the police, he built relationships with many officers, including the chief of police, who was known to visit Ruby's "special parties."

Ruby acted as his own bouncer and was always tough enough to take down the trouble-makers, drunks and other disruptive customers. He was known as a "fighter" and could be "brutal" if the circumstances needed him to be.

How and why Ruby and Oswald connected before the assassination is speculative, some say that Jack Ruby met up with Lee Harvey Oswald in early 1963, when Oswald was living and working in New Orleans, and passing out pro-Castro literature, but others claim there was a connection through the Mafia going back to when Oswald was a teenager.

Their connection strikes me as more than just happenstance, particularly as events unfolded later, Also, bear in mind the statements of Beverly Oliver, the 19-year-old stripper from the Colony Club, who talked about Ruby introducing her to Lee

Oswald at Ruby's club two weeks before the assassination. And then there is Oliver's description of a later meeting at Ruby's club among Ruby, Oswald, and Charles Harrelson among others. Was there a connection between Oswald and the man who killed him?

Ruby's last mugshot

My belief is that Ruby was asked to do just what he did: kill Oswald to keep him from telling the truth as he knew it. Those behind the assassination had no choice but to kill him, and it was Ruby they choose for that job. How they were able to convince him to be another "patsy" in this whole conspiracy may never be fully known, but there were many people who could not let the true story come out. Ruby told Warren Commission members Earl Warren and Gerald Ford that he feared for his life, but if they took him back to Washington he would tell them the entire story. They walked away. Even the Government didn't want the truth to be known.

You have to wonder why.

THREE TRAMPS

One of the many anomalies during the Nov. 22, 1963, assassination of President John F. Kennedy has to be the role played – if any – by three people, who have become known as the "Three Tramps" in the railroad yard.

When the shots rang out that afternoon in Dallas, onlookers and police officers reacted instantly. Many stood in disbelief, some fell to the ground in self-preservation but many of those close to the motorcade began running up the grassy knoll in response to shots they heard coming from that direction.

A crowd numbering more than 200 joined the officers who were trained for such reaction, but all were stopped when they reached the top of the knoll by men that, according to witnesses interviewed later, showed Secret Service badges and ordered the crowd back down to Dealey Plaza. All, including the police officers, turned around and went back the way they had come.

One of those in close proximity to the motorcade was Dallas Police Department motorcycle officer Bobbie Hargis. He was riding in a position to the left and behind the President's limousine. According to his testimony, which has been consistent over the years, he heard the shots, was splattered with blood and brain matter from the president, and reported that his first impression was that the shots had come from in front and to his right, in the direction of the grassy knoll and the railroad overpass. He laid his bike down and took off on foot with the crowd. He testified about the confusion and about running up the grassy knoll. Along with Hargis, the majority of the crowd firmly believed the shots they heard came from behind the stockade fence on the knoll, which is where they ran in what can best be described as a collective willingness to stop the shooter without giving thought to their own personal safety.

Just beyond that stockade fence was a railroad yard and, shortly after the assassination, Dallas Police officers arrested a number of suspicious vagrants, three of whom were found in an empty rail car and photographed as they were walked through Dealey Plaza on the way to police headquarters. Known as the "three tramps," they were eventually identified as Charles Frederick Rogers, Charles Harrelson and Chauncey Holt. Holt died in 1997; Harrelson died in 2007; and Rogers has disappeared. The

photos show three relatively clean-cut and properly dressed men looking less like tramps than regular people in casual clothes. The three were held for a short time, and then released, with almost no record made of their arrests, per Robert Groden's research in *The Killing of a President*. According to Chauncey Holt, it was Gordon Shanklin, the Special Agent in Charge of the FBI in Dallas, who released him and the other two "tramps."

There has been confusion about just who these men were, and part of that comes from the disclosure that investigators and members of the Warren Commission named two more sets of three persons and named them as being the "tramps" in question. Yet over the years, I have read a number of other publications in which Holt positively identified himself and the other two as the tramps. There are also instances over the years when Harrelson admitted to assassinating the president, only to retract those statements. With two of the three now dead and Rogers nowhere to be found, we may never know the truth of just how or if the tramps were part of an assassination conspiracy. What we do know is this:

Holt was an accountant for Meyer Lansky, a onetime, well-known mob financier. Holt was alleged to have said that he spent a great deal of time forging documents and doing other illegal chores for the CIA. He said he was ordered to Dallas before the assassination to deliver a number of fake Secret Service credentials. I suspect it was those credentials that were exhibited to several persons in the Dealey Plaza area. These credentials were later shown to be fake IDs, as the Secret Service said they had no agents stationed on the knoll, near the stockade fence or the railroad yard.

Holt said that he traveled to Dallas around the time of the assassination with Charles Nicoletti and Leo Moceri. Both Nicoletti and Moceri were contacted in the 1970s by the House Select Committee on Assassinations and were scheduled to testify before the committee. Nicoletti died suspiciously (three gunshots to the head and a car firebomb) before he was able to testify. Moceri disappeared.

Charles Nicoletti

I only knew *of* Nicoletti, but Leo Moceri I knew very well. Moceri lived in Akron, and I spent many, many long days and nights investigating "Lips" Moceri, with the intention of putting him in the penitentiary where he belonged. It was reported that every time Moceri left Akron, upon his return someone was dead. He was a contract killer for the mob, obviously with no compunctions about cold-blooded murder. Imagine my surprise during the research I've done for this book to find Moceri listed as a "person of interest."

Leo "Lips" Moceri

Moceri has disappeared, but I have no doubt that he is dead. Akron Police Department detectives Bob George, Dick Etling and I were conducting an investigation in 1976 which led us to the trunk of Moceri's Lincoln parked at a local hotel in Fairlawn Ohio. The one-inch carpet, golf shoes and clubs in that trunk were saturated with blood, and we knew immediately that Moceri was "done in." While his body was never recovered, Danny Green, another hoodlum we investigated, was well known to have put a hit out on Moceri.

Holt was 70 years old when he gave an interview that was published in a Jan. 14, 1992 *Globe* article, with the headline: "Mystery tramp charges: 'Cheers' star's dad shot Kennedy – and I gave him the gun." In the article, Holt reportedly

decided to "come clean," and admitted that he was the old man in the hat carrying a brown paper bag in the photo of the unknown tramps. He also identified Harrelson as the tall tramp and Rogers as the third tramp known as "Frenchie." Holt explains how the three of them were arrested in a railroad boxcar shortly after JFK's murder. He describes how the bag he was carrying in the photo contained a radio to monitor police activities, and it was that radio and fake Secret Service credentials – delivered by him to Dallas – that helped them slip through

Chauncey Holt - 1964

the fingers of justice, leaving Oswald to take the rap. The three were allegedly released after convincing the authorities that they were actually undercover agents assigned to protect the president.

According to Holt, Oswald was a "patsy," and years later Holt said Oswald got a raw deal. "I don't think its right for Oswald's children to suffer and live with a lie," he said in the article.

Additionally, Holt confirmed that Harrelson was a part of the assassination team, adding that he gave Harrelson a handgun and a fake Secret Service badge the morning of the assassination.

Harrelson was born in Huntsville, Texas, but moved as a young man to California, where he initially was an encyclopedia salesman. He later turned to crime as a way of life, and in 1960 he was convicted of armed robbery. Like Moceri, Harrelson was believed to be a contract killer.

Charles Harrelson - 1960

Harrelson was said to have murdered Sam Degelia in a contract killing in south Texas in 1968. He was convicted, served his time and was then released.

In 1979, drug dealers paid Harrelson $250,000 to assassinate Federal Judge John Wood, the first federal judge to be killed in the 20th century. When Harrelson was arrested for the murder of Wood, he confessed to being one of the gunmen that killed President Kennedy. Harrelson later withdrew that confession, was convicted of killing Judge Wood and sentenced to life in prison. He died there.

At one point while in prison, Harrelson was reportedly shown a photo of the "three tramps."

Harrelson

He looked at the photo and denied it was him. Then he looked at it again and said it did show a resemblance. At that point, he was alleged to have shown a slight smile, thrown

the photo on the table, got up and walked out of the interview.

I have studied photos of Harrelson and compared them to the "tramp photo." It is my belief that the second of the three men is Harrelson.

Charles Frederick Rogers, the first tramp in the photos taken that November afternoon, was born in 1921 and studied physics at the University of Houston. During the Second World War, Rogers served with the Organization of Naval Intelligence and supposedly became a member of the CIA in the mid-to-late 50s, which is around the same time that he became an

Charles Rogers

associate of Carlos Marcello, a known mobster in New Orleans.

In another twist of fate, there are photographs taken in New Orleans of what appears to be Holt and possibly Rogers with Lee Harvey Oswald, distributing pro-Castro pamphlets, supposedly on behalf of the CIA. Again, it is extraordinary to

Holt

think of the number of people connected directly or indirectly to the Kennedy assassination investigation that were said to have ties with the CIA.

Rogers has not been seen since 1965. That was when Houston

authorities went to the home belonging to his parents. They did not find Rogers, but as the officers were looking through the home, they made a gruesome discovery – the severed head of Rogers' mother in the vegetable drawer of the refrigerator. Authorities found that someone – and Rogers was the only suspect – had dismembered both his mother and father and stuffed them into the ice box in a case that became known as "The Ice Box Murders."

The supposition is that when his parents discovered his covert activities – including his part in the JFK assassination – he killed them to keep them quiet. After he disappeared, Rogers was reported still to be working for the CIA, although there is speculation that he was eventually murdered in Honduras.

There were many players in the assassination of President John Kennedy. I have expanded on the roles of just a few of them here, particularly the ones whose actions have led to more questions and skepticism on my part.

As hard as it is to imagine the disparate personalities coming together, there is a thread that binds them – the death of the president.

After all these years and all the myriad conspiracy theories, there is still no definitive truth – at least for me – about what really happened in Dallas on Nov. 22, 1963.

Chapter Twelve

A Full Investigation

As a rookie Special Agent for the FBI on November 22, 1963, I experienced some of the deepest anguish in my life. *Had I messed up?* The President was dead!

Then came the word that a Lee Harvey Oswald had been arrested ... not Joseph Adams Milteer. Whew! I had done my job and all I needed to do was find Milteer and ask my questions.

But as we all know, now, that wasn't quite true, and even after twenty years of investigation, searching through the National Archives and reading myriad books and articles on the case, I am still left wondering what actually happened. One thing I do believe is Lee Harvey Oswald didn't shoot the President of the United States.

So, if it wasn't Oswald, who was it and why?

I can't answer those questions, but I can add a bit more to the investigative materials that have been developed through the dedication of millions of fellow citizens searching for truth, and the redemption of our Republic.

From looking at the historical record and my personal experience with the investigation, it is clear that there were actions taken both before and after the assassination that clouded what was really going on.

After the assassination the record shows that there was much consternation about Oswald's Communist ties, with both the CIA and FBI delivering reports to LBJ the morning after, "strongly suggesting that Castro was behind the assassination." Professor Peter Dale Scott expounds online in an essay titled "Deep Politics III" that a two-phased operation was first used to scare people into jumping to a conclusion (lone nut), to cover up any inconvenient loose ends.

The Warren Commission was formed, and the case evidence was stolen and taken to Washington, D.C. After the "cover-up" was locked in place, the "sensitive information" was then "clarified" so as to make the initial Communist-conspiracy claim moot.

Senator Richard Russell of Georgia was unwilling to serve with Chief Justice Earl Warren, one reason being that he thought Warren would do anything for the publicity. So, at the end of his plea to Russell on Nov. 29, 1963, President Johnson tells how he got Earl Warren to serve: "… you want me to tell you the truth? You know what happened? Bobby [Kennedy] and them went up to see him today and he turned them down cold and said NO. Two hours later I called him and ordered him down here and he didn't want to come. I insisted he come … came down here and told me no twice and I just pulled out what Hoover told me about a little incident in Mexico City and I say now, I don't want Mr. Khruschev to be told tomorrow and be testifying before a camera that he killed this fellow … and that Castro killed him."

Earlier in Johnson's pitch to get Russell to accept service on the Commission, he plays the nuclear-holocaust card, "… we've got to take this out of the arena where they're testifying that Khruschev and Castro did this and did that and check us into a war that can kill 40 million Americans in an hour."

Later, after the witness recanted and sensitive information was declared to be spurious, Oswald was entrenched firmly in the role of lone-nut assassin. A pristine bullet that delivered multiple wounds was invented, the Warren Commission was released and, supposedly, our national nightmare was over.

The excuse of Communist entanglement and where that may lead was brought up in a Letterhead Memo to FBI Asst. Director Alan Belmont on Nov. 22, 1963 informing him of a call from Deputy Attorney General Nicholas Katzenbach that came in at 5:09 P.M. saying, "… if it develops that Oswald is the man who did it, the assassination or was involved in it, his pro-Cuban and pro-Soviet activities will come into mounting prominence."

Katzenbach also wrote a memo to Bill Moyers early on November 25, the day after Oswald was shot, where he declared,

"Speculation about Oswald's motivation ought to be cut off, and we should have some basis for rebutting thought that this was a Communist conspiracy or (as the Iron Curtain press is saying) a right wing conspiracy to blame it on the Communist."

This type of thinking may help explain some of the "official" lies and fraud that surround my investigation into Milteer, but it only accentuates that the monkey business before the assassination is very suspicious, possibly even sinister – portending foreknowledge.

On page three of a Nov. 11, 1963 the Secret Service report about Milteer's threat of two days earlier, there is a "request" from the Protective Research Section regarding the President's safety during the upcoming trip to Miami: "SAIC [Robert] Bouck requested that the appropriate offices ... make discreet inquiries concerning these individuals on the FBI level and only of trusted enforcement agencies known to have *no sympathies feelings or alignments with organization such as the Klu Klux Klan or other radical right wing organizations* [emphasis added]."

This shows that there was some official concern about sympathizers in the ranks. Was that the reason I was not told about the Nov. 9 tape recorded threats, and then had my reports rigged? Was I simply a Yankee in Johnny Reb country? Were fellow agents simply covering up a good-old-boy network?

Or did Milteer actually know something, and did forces conspire to make sure he was not truly interviewed about the assassination. Or was there a combination of circumstances and reasons? Again, I have to sadly say, I do not know.

President Kennedy may have been alive when he left Dallas if proper procedures had been followed. There is also no doubt that destroying evidence and lying about it impacted the FBI investigation into the President's death, at the very least calling into question the completeness and validity of the Warren Commission Report.

The United States of America and John F. Kennedy deserve a new and full investigation.

The official portrait of the 35th President of the United States

Time to Begin

The assassination of John Fitzgerald Kennedy was one of the most consequential events of the 20th century. It changed history.

I conclude that, in the early 1960s, an unknown number of powerful people came together and held private discussions. These discussions centered on the bitterness and hatred they felt towards President Kennedy, and on how to eliminate him.

That they could have contemplated doing something of this magnitude was unconscionable. To do what they did took masterful planning and manipulation. The fact that they accomplished it without paying the consequences tells us that they were successful. Now, almost 50 years later, we still know very little of the actual details of the plot, due to the oppressive weight of the Warren Commission's pre-emptive conclusions, and commentary by so-called experts, who ignore or dismiss mountains of evidence to the contrary.

As the 50th anniversary of this great tragedy approaches, it is time to begin again. Americans and people around the world have the right to know as much of the truth as can be learned.

We, as Americans, need to demand that this be done, so that our slaughtered President, John Fitzgerald Kennedy, can finally rest in peace.

My name is Donald A. Adams, F.B.I., Retired, and this is my testimony.

In 1995, former FBI Agent Don Adams went to the National Archives and was troubled to find that official reports he generated in 1963 were missing. Information from those reports was found inserted into other agents reports ... and bold lies were told about the whereabouts of a man who had threatened to kill President Kennedy.

Afterword

by Harrison E. Livingstone

Don Adams presents crucial information in this book that furthers the investigation of President Kennedy's assassination and should be considered in the light of long-time government lies and cover-ups. The government's Official Story of the assassination was exploded long ago by careful studies of the evidence, but rarely do we find someone like Don Adams who has been inside an investigation, let alone one that had looked at the murder of a president. Adams exposes lies and deceit dealing with evidence that tends to implicate powerful elements of the government in burying material we should consider.

This book shows people not familiar with the case, as well as specialists in the general evidence of the murder, some new aspects that point directly to an official cover-up. Since Don Adams has personal knowledge of official lying about where Joseph Adams Milteer was on the day of the assassination, this is the first great contribution of his book. Milteer, a radical extremist, was always a suspect in researchers' minds because he was tape recorded by the police in a long discussion about what appeared to be the assassination before it took place. Adams worked with the FBI in Georgia, the same state where Milteer lived, and had been assigned to investigate him just after the shooting to determine where he was when it took place. The FBI has attempted to insist that Milteer was at home and not in Dallas, but Adams has been able to show that Milteer may well have been in Dallas on the day of the murder, and further, Adams tracked fabricated evidence implicating FBI operatives in covering it up. Why would they want to do this?

After his retirement, when Adams voiced concerns about the Warren Report, researcher Deanie Richards sent him a copy of a U.S. Secret Service document in the National Archives dealing with the FBI's assertion that Milteer was in Quitman, GA at the time of the assassination, verification of what was written in an earlier FBI teletype. The Letterhead Memorandum covers the period from November 22 to November 25, 1963, and deals with ascertaining the whereabouts of known suspects or persons who had made alleged threats against the President.

Researcher Jeff Caufield provided Adams with documentation of an undated memorandum to Cartha DeLoach, re: "Assassination of President John F. Kennedy." DeLoach was very close to J. Edgar Hoover. The first paragraph reads: "Following the assassination of President Kennedy on 11/22/63, Milteer, because of his known association with hate-type organizations and his previous threat regarding President Kennedy, was immediately considered a suspect. However, our investigation determined he was in Quitman, Georgia, his home, on 11-22-63"

Adams asks this question: "How did an "Agent in Thomasville" verify that Milteer was in Quitman, Georgia, on Nov. 22, 1963, the day of the assassination of President Kennedy?" Adams also describes a photograph well known to researchers that apparently shows Milteer in Dealey Plaza during the motorcade that carried the president to his death. Adams presents many pieces of personal testimony: "Royal McGraw had been with me when I received the orders from Atlanta FBI office to go find Milteer for the Secret Service.... I firmly believe that Milteer could have been discovered in Dallas at the time of the killing of the President.

"This would have caused the investigation to snowball, and all of the information that both agencies had in their hands would have surfaced. That would certainly have changed the course of history!"

Adams says, "I can state unequivocally that Milteer was not in Georgia on Nov. 22; I was looking for him, and he was not to be found until five days later....

"With all that was then known, Milteer and his associates should have been held and charged on a conspiracy violation. They might have been, had not the lies deflected attention from Milteer, and had Oswald not been arrested and silenced shortly thereafter. This cemented Oswald's alleged guilt and ended all other investigations."

I was always suspicious of the Milteer story in the JFK evidence, and wrote about it now and then, though not at first voicing my suspicions. I thought that the story was invented to deflect attention to radical right wingers and away from the military and intelligence operatives with a Texas background who were involved in the conspiracy. Unwittingly, Adams backed up my misgivings when he quotes Milteer allegedly saying after the assassination, to William Somersett, a long-time government informant that "everything ran true to form. I guess you thought I was kidding you when I said he would be killed from a window with a high-powered rifle." What is wrong with this? The alleged murder weapon in evidence, the Mannlicher-Carcano 6.5, was a medium-to-low-powered rifle, and notoriously faulty and dangerous to shooters. The FBI's own firearms expert, Robert Frazier, told the Warren Commission that the bullet was traveling at only 1800 FPS (feet per second), whereas a high powered rifle must develop 3000 FPS and could be capable of 4100 FPS, *if* the Mannlicher was indeed the murder weapon. Of course, high-powered weapons could have been involved.

What this means is that Milteer had no knowledge of the weapon or probably no real knowledge of what happened, since it tends to establish that there was in fact (in line with the Official Story of a shooter from behind the limousine) that the shots had been fired from the Texas School Book Depository, a *warehouse* which was far from being an "office building."

There was major evidence indicating that Oswald was in the 2nd floor lunchroom with not enough time for him to get there after the last shot, and that no one fired from the building because nearly all of its employees had been standing in front of the building after the motorcade passed, and they turned and reentered the building, which they would not have done had someone been firing from a window. All the rest of the available evidence indicated that either shots came from the Grassy Knoll alongside the car, or from manholes on the overpass facing it as the car approached from the East.

So, for me, the entire Milteer story was a plant for the above stated reasons. But I went along with it under intense pressure from certain persons in the research who later turned out to be indeed planting false evidence in the case, including some of the biggest hoaxes of our time.

Adams tells us about his encounter with Milteer five days after the assassination. But Adams was limited to only five questions dictated by FBI SAC James McMahon, and thus prevented from asking him if he had been in Dallas that 22 November.

Adams tells us that his investigative 302 [FBI Report] on Milteer is missing from the National Archives. Of course there is nothing much new in this case along the lines of missing evidence. We discovered this long ago when there was a Texan in charge of the original hard evidence such as the "Magic Bullet" at the National Archives (CE 399). Adams says that also missing is the hate material and other data he obtained from Milteer in his background investigation.

I published the transcript of the taped discussion between Milteer and his boyhood friend, Willie Somersett, in Appendix B of *High*

Treason. At the time I was inclined to believe that it might in fact be a conspiratorial meeting, but was always leery of it, and now, what do you think it might mean? This is what it says:

> **Somersett:** Well, how in the hell do you figure would be the best way to get him?
> **Milteer:** From an office building with a high-powered rifle.
> …
> **Somersett:** You think he knows he is a marked man?
> **Milteer:** Sure he does.
> **Somersett:** They are really going to try to kill him?
> **Milteer:** Oh, yeah. It is in the works." Brown [Jack Brown, a Ku Klux Klan Imperial Wizard] himself, Brown is just as likely to get him as anybody in the world. He hasn't said so, but he tried to get Martin Luther King.
> **Somersett:** Hitting this Kennedy is gonna be a hard proposition, I tell you. I believe you may have figured out a way to get him, the office building and all that. I don't know how the Secret Service agents cover all them office buildings everywhere he is going. Do you know whether they do that or not?
> **Milteer:** Well, if they have any suspicion they do that, of course. But without suspicion, chances are they won't.

There is more to this discussion about how to get the rifle up to the window in pieces and what to do when the murder has happened, which is to be "Ready," and on "Go." Presumably, they already knew what to do if JFK was shot. Or so they thought, their "revolutionary" group was shot full of informers, such as Somersett and many other spies.

Is Milteer for real? Or is he just another mindless hate-filled idiot blowing in the wind?

Don Adams has questions too, and asks, "Was Milteer a conspirator, or just prophetic, foretelling the assassination of JFK? He was hardly a prophet, but just how involved he really was, we may never know. Like so many others connected to the assassination investigation, Milteer died a mysterious death."

Adams asks these cogent questions: "Why, with all we suspect about Milteer now, doesn't the government, the Dallas Police Department or a duly empowered panel of experts, using all of the techniques, technology and investigative skills available today, go back to square one and start over? Murder is never a closed case until it is solved."

Ken Thompson, writing in the *The Fourth Decade*, a journal of assassination research once edited and published by Prof. Jerry Rose, at the University of New York at Fredonia, suggested that Milteer, had to have been involved in the JFK conspiracy because he seemed to know that the murder was about to happen. Milteer was of great interest to all those who were on track of a *low level* Right Wing conspiracy. Ken Thompson suggested, as Christopher Sharrett writes, that the Milteer tapes are a "valid pointer to the source of the true assassination conspiracy." Sharrett has a prescient comment about this: "I suggest that these provocative tapes, which have been in the public's hands for years, were another small attempt to divert public attention from the state's implication in the assassination."

Sharrett, a professor of media and journalism at Seton Hall University, a long-time Kennedy assassination researcher, wrote a very fine article in *The Fourth Decade*, and was a proponent of the theory that the assassination was a state crime. He is close to the position of John Judge and a few others who think it came from the Joint Chiefs of the Armed Services. The government admitted that the Central Intelligence Agency (CIA) was working with organized crime figures to try to assassinate Fidel Castro, the Prime Minister of Cuba, and there were other examples of collaboration with criminal syndicates in various endeavors both patriotic and sometimes for pure profit in the drug trade. I was trying to see what it meant in a broader sense, in terms of a massive conspiracy that involved faking the autopsy evidence and hiding a big ambush in Dealey Plaza that fateful day.

The theorists of the assassination as a state crime do not come out and say whether or not the Establishment was directly involved or merely condoned or tacitly approved the assassination. The term "Establishment" then has to be defined, and by that I mean who would have orchestrated the murder? Does it mean that it originated in intelligence agencies or circles, or that of the military? In the bureaucracy?

I have no doubt that some of our modern robber barons with plenty of money have a criminal character, but it is not plausible that any such conspiracy among civilian government and the military could ever have been perpetrated without the agreement and knowledge of a significant segment of the establishment, even regional in character, such as Texas based. Although many among the rich and powerful may be ultra-conservative, most are upright people who draw the line at violence, and for the most part wish to preserve at least the semblance of democracy. They are aware that they themselves might just as easily become victims, as happened in the French Revolution and many other upheavals and coups which began to feed on themselves. It was the loyal Establishment *and* the general public that had to be duped.

Carlos Marcello or Santos Trafficante could not kill the president without the agreement of the National Syndicate, which was most likely considering the potential backlash, and most unlikely because the cover-up was from within the government, powerful military and national police (FBI). The Mob would have written their own death warrant had they killed JFK alone.

Clearly the evidence framing Oswald was planted primarily by Dallas police and FBI, though all of it may not have originated with them. Oswald was set up in advance, as Don Adams suspects, which you'll read in this book.

My best explanation of the assassination remains that put forward by those who postulated a "Yankee/Cowboy" war. We continue to have a cultural war raging in the United States between the Right and the Center, and the Northern half of the U.S. and some elements in the South. It is a great misfortune that Right Wing radicals have succeeded in labeling anyone a little toward center (or between them and the center) "Leftists." As everyone who has ever been the victim of labeling knows, one's fate is often writ in a misnomer. In this country, the large majority are in the center, neither Left nor Right, thankfully. They are the ones that are hurt the most—as those caught in the middle often are. We are not really a polarized nation, in spite of the best efforts of those who would radicalize us.

Certainly elements of the National Security State, such as some in various agencies of government, and in various extra-governmental outfits and alliances, were used in the conspiracy. But just as surely, the conspiracy that murdered John Kennedy came from Texas and their allies in all the above agencies and the military. Renegade agents in the CIA, for example, the very dangerous Texan, David Atlee Phillips, joined in a common cause with fellow Texans in the military and with J. Edgar Hoover at the FBI to kill Kennedy and cover it up. For the most part, they had foreknowledge of the plot.

Christopher Sharrett writes, "The evidence in the assassination of John Kennedy was taken control of and represented to the public by those sectors of state and private power who truly despised Kennedy and his policies. It is true that Mafia types and various exile groupings appear within the assassination scenario. These same groups appear within the Watergate and Iran/Contra. Does appreciating the presence of these groups go very far to aid our understanding of these events as state crimes, in fact as crimes against the Constitution and the people of the U.S. carried out by state authority?"

I think that the above comment says it as well as anyone who truly knows the evidence in President Kennedy's heinous murder ever could.

Harrison Edward Livingstone
Best-Selling Author
High Treason: The Assassination of JFK & the Case for Conspiracy;
High Treason 2; Killing Kennedy: And the Hoax of the Century;
Killing the Truth: Deceit and Deception in the JFK Case

Documents

-2-

On November 24th, after the news came through that Ruby had shot Oswald, according to Somersett, Milterr told them "all clear, don't worry".

Milterr's account of the shooting in Dallas is that Ruby shot from the Mall and that Tippett shot from the top of a building. A good guess is that this was the Baltex Building. Milterr was not clear about Oswald's role although he thought he was downstairs in the book depository rather than on the upper floor. Somersett guesses that it might have been Milterr himself that fired the shots from the windows of the book depositor. As to the killing of Tippett, it is Somersett's belief that Oswald knew that Tippett was going to kill him, so he shot Tippett first. Tippett apparently did not know that Oswald was armed.

In the recorded conversation of November 9th, mention was made of a man by the name of Bond from Chattanooga. This is Jack Bond, the grand dragon of the Tennessee clan who owned either a welding or machine shop. He was involved in a number of killings and he has a son named Gerald who is now head of the Tennessee clan.

Somersett remarkably enough was also involved in a prediction of the shooting of Martin Luther King. He had been to a labor meeting in New York where there had been much talk of King's muscling in on labor leaders in the Memphis situation. He overheard a conversation that King would be killed if he came back to Memphis and kept fiddling with the labor problems. The day before King was shot, Somersett told several people at a local Miami garage that the shooting would take place next evening. When the shooting did take place, he went back and verified it with the people at the garage and this is known to the man in the Intelligence Unit.

Somersett has worked for some years as an informant to the FBI. At the moment, he is not in their good graces because of his refusal to keep still about the various assassination problems. He is also in difficulty with Milterr because as a result of some conversations, Mr. William Baggs, the Editor of the Miami News went to talk with Milterr who was very put out at the fact that the story had been made public.

This is the second page of the June 5, 1968, memorandum shown on page 97. A copy of this conversation, tape recorded by the Miami Police Department Intelligence Unit, was provided immediately to the FBI. Discussions centered on Milteer not only being interested in killing President Kennedy but also Martin Luther King Jr. The memorandum outlines what Somersett knew about the alibi Milteer had set up for his trip to Dallas; how Milteer told him that Jack Ruby had shot Lee Harvey Oswald and that now was "all clear don't worry"; that in Milteer's account of the shooting in Dallas, Ruby shot from the mall and Tippit (no reference about whether this is the Officer Tippit who was also shot and killed that day) shot from the top of a building; and how Milteer was not clear about Oswald's role although he thought Oswald was downstairs in the Texas School Book Depository at the time of the shooting. The memorandum continues by stating that Somersett was also involved in a prediction of the shooting of Martin Luther King Jr., but that Somersett was not in "good graces" with the FBI "because of his refusal to keep still about the various assassination problems."

URGENT   1:45 AM EST 11-17-63 HLF   1 PAGE

TO   ALL SACS

FROM DIRECTOR

THREAT TO ASSISINATE PRESIDENT KENNEDY IN DALLAS TEXAS

NOVEMBER TWENTYTWO DASH TWENTYTHREE NINETEEN SIXTYTHREE.

MISC INFORMATION CONCERNING.

INFO HAS BEEN RECEIVED BY THE BUREAU

BUREAU HAS ~~DISSEMIERREXIIRFAMATION~~ DETERMINED THAT A MILITANT

REVOLUTIONARY GROUP MAY ATTEMPT TO ASSINATED PRESIDENT

KENNEDY ON HIS PROPOSED TRIP TO DALLAS TEXAS ~~EMRIX&XTREX~~

~~XMREXXGRX~~ NOVEMBER TWENTYTWO DASH TWENTYTHREE NINETEEN

SICTYTHREE.

ALL RECEIVING OFFICE SHOULS IMMIDIATELY CONTACT ALL CIS;

PCIS LOGICAL RACIAL AND HATE GROPUP INFORMANTS AND DETERMINE IF

ANY BASIS FOR THREAT. BHRGEU SHOULS BE KEPT ADVISED OF ALL

DEVELOPEMENTS BY TELETYPE .

   SUBMIY FD THREE ZERO TWOS AND LHM

OTHER HOFFICE HAVE BEEN ADVISED

END AND ACK PLS

   MO.....
   DL......

NO.....

KT TI TU CLR..@

A November 17, 1963 FBI Teletype telling of a threat to assassinate the President in Dallas on the 22nd by a "militant revolutionary group." For some time the Bureau denied the existence of this threat. Again, why was the president allowed to ride in an open car in such a hostile environment?

UNITED STATES GOVERNMENT

Memorandum

TO : MR. DELMONT

DATE: November 22, 1963

FROM : S. B. DONAHOE

SUBJECT: ASSASSINATION OF THE PRESIDENT

Deputy Attorney General Katzenbach called at 5:09 p.m. He said he realized that things were happening very fast and he was calling to ask that he be kept informed if there are going to be any arrests of the person or persons who assassinated the President. In other words, he would like to be advised when it is apparent there is going to be a solution.

The Deputy Attorney General also commented that if it develops that Oswald is the man who did the assassination or was involved in it, then his pro-Cuban and pro-Soviet activities will come into mounting prominence. He said if Oswald is so identified, the State Department should be advised as there are definite foreign policy considerations and decisions here.

Assistant Deputy Attorney General William A. Geoghegan called at 5:15 p.m. on behalf of the Deputy Attorney General. He advised that two men in the State Department have definite coordination responsibility in connection with any State Department action which would be required, if it develops that Oswald is implicated in the assassination. If this implication develops State Department will need full details on Oswald's background. The people at State Department to be notified in this regard are as follows:

    John Crimmins   OR   William Bowdler
    Extension 4588   Extension 3736
    Home phone FR 4-6151   Home Phone FE 7-4712

I emphasized to Geoghegan that he must recognize, and I am sure the Deputy Attorney General so understood, that we could not give out any blow-by-blow account of what is happening and that we would only be acting in this regard when it became apparent that the solution is imminent. He was in agreement.

Our reports on Oswald are in the possession of State Department and Supervisor E.T. Turner of the Domestic Intelligence Division is so advising Crimmins or Bowdler tonight.

SBD:hmc
(6)

1 - Belmont
1 - Evans
1 - Rosen
1 - Sullivan
1 - Donahoe

A November 22, 1963 FBI Letterhead Memorandum shows immediate concern about Oswald's pro-Soviet and pro-Cuban activities.

November 25, 1963

MEMORANDUM FOR MR. MOYERS

It is important that all of the facts
surrounding President Kennedy's Assassination be
made public in a way which will satisfy people in
the United States and abroad that all the facts
have been told and that a statement to this effect
to made now.

1. The public must be satisfied that
Oswald was the assassin; that he did not have
confederates who are still at large; and that
the evidence was such that he would have been
convicted at trial.

2. Speculation about Oswald's motivation
ought to be cut off, and we should have some basis
for rebutting thought that this was a Communist
conspiracy or (as the Iron Curtain press is saying)
a right-wing conspiracy to blame it on the Communists.
Unfortunately the facts on Oswald seem about too pat--
too obvious (Marxist, Cuba, Russian wife, etc.). The
Dallas police have put out statements on the Communist
conspiracy theory, and it was they who were in charge
when he was shot and thus silenced.

3. The matter has been handled thus far
with neither dignity nor conviction. Facts have been
mixed with rumour and speculation. We can scarcely
let the world see us totally in the image of the
Dallas police when our President is murdered.

I think this objective may be satisfied
by making public as soon as possible a complete and
thorough FBI report on Oswald and the assassination.
This may run into the difficulty of pointing to inconsistencies between this report and statements by
Dallas police officials. But the reputation of the
Bureau is such that it may do the whole job.

The only other step would be the appointment
of a Presidential Commission of unimpeachable personnel
to review and examine the evidence and announce its
conclusions. This has both advantages and disadvantages.
It think it can await publication of the FBI report
and public reaction to it here and abroad.

I think, however, that a statement that
all the facts will be made public property in an
orderly and responsible way should be made now. We
need something to head off public speculation or
Congressional hearings of the wrong sort.

Nicholas deB. Katzenbach
Deputy Attorney General

A November 25, 1963 memorandum from Nicholas Katzenbach to LBJ spokes-
person Bill Moyers laying down the reasons for a cover-up.

FEDERAL BUREAU OF INVESTIGATION

REPORTING OFFICE	OFFICE OF ORIGIN	DATE	INVESTIGATIVE PERIOD	
ATLANTA	ATLANTA	1/22/64	1/13 - 14/64	
TITLE OF CASE		**REPORT MADE BY**		**TYPED BY**
JOSEPH ADAMS MILTEER		SA ROYAL A. McGRAW		sda
		CHARACTER OF CASE		
ALL INFORMATION CONTAINED HEREIN IS UNCLASSIFIED DATE 7-1-94 BY		RACIAL MATTERS		

REFERENCE: Bureau airtel to Atlanta, 12/12/63, entitled "Constitutional American Parties of the U. S., RM."

- P -

ENCLOSURES: TO BUREAU

One photograph of subject.

LEADS:

BALTIMORE, BIRMINGHAM, DALLAS, HOUSTON, JACKSONVILLE, KNOXVILLE, SAVANNAH AND WASHINGTON FIELD OFFICE

One copy each of this report is being furnished the above offices inasmuch as MILTEER has visited or contacted persons living within these divisions.

APPROVED	SPECIAL AGENT IN CHARGE	DO NOT WRITE IN SPACES BELOW
COPIES MADE:		157 / 1223 - 3 REC- 12
5- Bureau (Enc.) (RM)		
3- Atlanta (157-608)		11 JAN 24 1964
ADDITIONAL COPIES COVER PAGE B		

58 FEB 5 1964

DISSEMINATION RECORD OF ATTACHED REPORT		NOTATIONS
AGENCY	CRS-Y3 R-2 55	
REQUEST RECD.		
DATE FWD.	2/3/64	
HOW FWD.		
BY		

1 cc sent to Crim Div bu 6-94 2/3/64

The full 26-page January 22, 1964 report of Royal McGraw (pp. 176-201). Even though this report contains more information about Milteer and his relationship to the assassination, Harding's December 1, 1963 report was used as *the* report for information about Milteer by investigative bodies.

AT 157-608

ADDITIONAL COPIES

        1- Baltimore (Info) (RM)
        1- Birmingham (Info) (RM)
        1- Dallas (Info) (RM)
        1- Houston (Info)(RM)
        1- Jacksonville (Info) (RM)
        1- Knoxville (Info) (RM)
        2- Miami (RM)
        1- Savannah (Info) (RM)
        1- WFO (Info) (RM)

LEADS: (Continued)

    MIAMI

        AT MIAMI, FLORIDA

            Will maintain contact with WILLIAM SOMERSETT,
    former Miami 607-C (RAC). ʸ

        ATLANTA

            AT QUITMAN AND VALDOSTA, GEORGIA

                Will follow activities of JOSEPH ADAMS MILTEER
    in connection with his forming the Constitutional American
    Parties of the United States. ʸ

INFORMANTS:

Identity of Source	File Where Located
T-1 is AT 1691-C (RAC)	157-414 137-1325A
T-2 is WILLIAM SOMERSETT former Miami 607-C (RAC)	105-208 157-414 157-608

T-3 is ROBERT GORDON
  Anti-Defamation League
  Indianapolis, Indiana
	105-280

- B -
(COVER PAGE)

*2 copies made
for review at FBIHQ by
HSC-A Committee
JTALE 5/30/77
Re: Somersett*

AT 157-608

Identity of Source	File Where Located
T-4 is IP 3161-C (RAC)	105-280
T-5 is SV 320-C (RAC)	157-608

SOURCES:

Neighborhood

Chief WILLIAM R. ELLIOTT, Quitman, Georgia, Police Department.

ADMINISTRATIVE:

Atlanta has no Bureau approved Thumbnail Sketch of the Constitution Party of the United States or the Constitutional American Parties of the United States. WILLIAM SOMERSETT, former Miami 607-C (RAC) advised MILTEER became disillusioned with the Constitution Party of the United States after attending a convention of this party at Indianapolis, Indiana, during October, 1963. Because of this MILTEER allegedly stated he was forming the Constitutional American Parties of the United States.

(COVER PAGE)

RELEASED PER P.L-102-526(JFK ACT)
NARA _BRh_ DATE _4-21-07_

FD-204 (Rev. . .)

UNITED STATES DEPARTMENT OF JUSTICE
FEDERAL BUREAU OF INVESTIGATION

Copy to:

Report of: SA ROYAL A. McGRAW   Office: Atlanta, Georgia
Date: January 22, 1964

Field Office File #: 157-608   Bureau File #:

Title: JOSEPH ADAMS MILTEER

ALL INFORMATION CONTAINED
HEREIN IS UNCLASSIFIED
DATE _7-1-94_ BY _SP8MAC/EH_
(JFK)

Character: RACIAL MATTERS

Synopsis: JOSEPH ADAMS MILTEER was born 2/26/02, at Quitman,
Ga., and presently lives at Quitman and Valdosta, Ga. MILTEER
is a wealthy bachelor who inherited an estimated $200,000 from
his father's estate. He has no family, no employment, and
spends a great deal of time travelling throughout the Southeast.
MILTEER has been unsuccessful in city politics at Quitman and
publishes a weekly pamphlet criticizing the operation of the
Quitman City Government. MILTEER has associated himself with
the Constitution Party of the U. S. and attended a convention
of this party held at Indianapolis, Ind., during October, 1963.
He was reprimanded by this party for describing himself as
being the party regional chairman for the Southeastern states.
MILTEER became disillusioned with the Constitution Party of
the U. S. and has attempted to form a party known as the
Constitutional American Parties of the U. S. MILTEER allegedly
intends to use the Constitutional American Parties of the U. S.
as a front to form a hard core underground for possible violence
in combating integration. MILTEER, on 11/9/63, was in a
conversation concerning the possible assassination of President
JOHN F. KENNEDY. MILTEER, on interview, admitted being a member
of the White Citizens Council, Atlanta, Ga., Congress of Freedom,
and the Constitution Party of the U. S. He denied making threats
to assassinate the President of the U. S. or participating in
the President's assassination. MILTEER REPORTEDLY CARRIES A .38
CALIBER REVOLVER IN HIS CAR WHEN TRAVELLING AND CAUTION SHOULD
BE USED IN EVENT MILTEER IS CONTACTED.

- P -

NSC-A Committee
_5/22/77_
Re: Somerset

DETAILS:

This document contains neither recommendations nor conclusions of the FBI. It is the property of the FBI and is loaned to
your agency; it and its contents are not to be distributed outside your agency.

AT 157-608

I. BACKGROUND

    A. Birthdate

        MILTEER, on November 27, 1963, advised he was born on February 26, 1902, at Quitman, Georgia. Records, Brooks County Health Department, and Brooks County Ordinary, Quitman, as examined on January 7, 1964, contained no record of MILTEER's birth. Records, Quitman High School, Quitman, Georgia, contain no birth data for MILTEER.

    B. Citizenship Status

        born at Quitman, Georgia

    C. Education

        Graduated from Quitman High School, Quitman, Georgia, in 1921.

    D. Marital Status

        Single

    E. Military Service

        MILTEER not known to have been in the Armed Forces of the United States.

    F. Credit and Identification

        ELEANOR L. POWERS, Credit Bureau of Brooks County, Quitman, Georgia, on September 24, 1962, advised she is personally acquainted with JOSEPH ADAMS MILTEER, who lives at the corner of Lafayette and Clay Streets, Quitman. MILTEER is considered to be an eccentric person and very little is known concerning his activities. He is approximately sixty years old and lives alone in a large run-down house. Very little is known concerning his background, but he was brought up in Quitman. His parents are deceased and he has no other relatives living in this area. It is rumored that MILTEER has lived in California and in the vicinity of Washington, D. C., where he operated some kind of concession around military reservations.

- 2 -

AT 157-608

MILTEER has never bought anything on credit and does most of his buying in Valdosta, Georgia. MILTEER is a very frugal person and his net worth is estimated to be in excess of $200,000. His father died approximately one year ago, leaving him a substantial amount of money and property. It has been rumored that MILTEER has made large deposits of money at banks in Jacksonville, Florida. During May, 1962, MILTEER sold the city of Quitman property for which he received $20,000 in cash.

POWERS advised a short time ago she visited the Minicipal Airport at Valdosta, Georgia. During this visit, she observed MILTEER hauling mail from the airport to the Post Office in Valdosta. She did not know whether he was an employee of the Post Office or whether he had a contract to haul mail. Other than the above, he is seemingly unemployed.

During the past few years, MILTEER has been a constant fault-finder in the management of the City of Quitman. He digs up insignificant things that have not been done properly by city officials and publishes a small leaflet criticising the city administration. He does not have any close friends and she had never heard of him meeting with any group or organization.

POWERS advised MILTEER is single and lives alone. There have been rumors that he was an associate of a woman in Valdosta, Georgia, but POWERS did not know the identity of this woman. She also heard that MILTEER was once arrested by the Valdosta, Georgia Police Department. Apparently nothing ever came of this arrest since MILTEER has never served a prison sentence to her knowledge. POWERS did not know the nature of the above arrest.

Records of the Credit Bureau of Brooks County, Quitman, Georgia, and the Credit Bureau of Valdosta, Valdosta, Georgia, as examined on January 7, 1964, revealed nothing in addition to the above information.

Chief WILLIAM R. ELLIOTT, Quitman, Georgia Police Department, on September 24, 1962, and January 7, 1964, advised MILTEER has no identification record with this department. _U_

- 3 -

AT   157-608

        Records of the Valdosta, Georgia Police Department
show MILTEER was arrested on January 29, 1955, on suspicion
of burglary and was released. He was fingerprinted on January
29, 1955, by the Lowndes County Sheriff's Office, Valdosta,
Georgia, Number 1153.

        The Identification Division, on December 2, 1963,
advised its records contained a duplicate of the above
fingerprint card and has no additional identification record
for MILTEER.

        G.   Employment

        MILTEER has no known employment at the present time.
ELEANOR L. POWERS, Credit Bureau of Brooks County, Quitman,
Georgia, advised MILTEER allegedly operated concessions in
the vicinity of military reservations in the past. She could
furnish no specific information concerning this employment.

        Confidential Informant AT T-2, on November 9, 1963,
advised MILTEER claimed to have been employed for three and
one-half years around the United States Supreme Court,
Washington, D. C. T-2 could furnish no specific information
concerning this alleged employment.

        J. A. McLEOD, Postmaster, Valdosta, Georgia, on
January 7, 1964, advised that around 1962 J. P. COFIELD,
Valdosta, Georgia, had a contract to haul mail from the
Municipal Airport, Valdosta, Georgia, to the Valdosta Post
Office. COFIELD was ill for two or three months during 1962
and had MILTEER substitute for him in hauling the above mail.
COFIELD no longer has the above contract.

        H.   Residence

1.   Corner of Clay and Lafayette Streets,
          Quitman, Georgia

2.   In care of Mrs. C. C. COFIELD
          212 South Troupe Street
          Valdosta, Georgia

- 4 -

AT 157-608

I.   Physical Description

The following is a physical description of MILTEER as obtained by interview and observation on November 27, 1963:

Name	JOSEPH ADAMS MILTEER
Race	White
Sex	Male
Height	5'4"
Weight	160 pounds
Eyes	Blue
Hair	Gray, partially thinning
Complexion	Ruddy
Characteristics	Wears glasses with metal frame; heavy waistline, small, round shouldered; nearly always unshaven, short gray stub with about two days growth, shabby dresser, wears old-fashioned clothes; tan hunting type cap; short legged; most of height from waist upward
Relatives	None known
FBI Number	None

J.   Make and Model of Automobile

1.   1962 gray Volvo, 1963 Georgia license 61-D 226

Records of the Brooks County Tax Collector, Quitman, Georgia, show 1963 Georgia 61-D 226 was issued February 22, 1963, to J. A. MILTEER, North Clay Street, Quitman, Georgia, for use on a 1962 Volvo, two-door sedan, Vehicle Identification Number 141502678.

2.   1963 Volkswagen station wagon, 1963 Georgia license 11D 2762

Records of the Lowndes County Tax Collector, Valdosta, Georgia, show 1963 Georgia license 11-D 2762 was issued on August 15, 1963, to JOE MILTEER, 212 South Troupe Street, Valdosta, Georgia, for use on a 1963 Volkswagen station wagon, model 221, Vehicle Identification Number 1043319. This Volkswagen was purchased on August 15, 1963, from Pipkins Motors, Inc., North Ashley Street, Valdosta, Georgia.

- 5 -

AT 157-608

EMMETT PIPKINS, Pipkins Motors, Inc., North Ashley Street, Valdosta, Georgia, on January 8, 1964, advised that MILTEER, on November 26, 1963, traded the above 1963 Volkswagen station wagon for a 1964 Volkswagen station wagon, Vehicle Identification Number 1185675, Motor Number 0312846. At the time of this trade MILTEER listed his address as 212 South Troupe Street, Valdosta, Georgia. The Volkswagen which is turquoise and white in color, bore no license place when observed by FBI Agents on November 27, 1963.

K. Photograph

MILTEER was photographed by FBI Agents on November 27, 1963, and copies of this photograph are maintained by Atlanta.

L. Special Abilities

MILTEER is a prolific writer and is the author of numerous pamphlets which he distributes himself.

MILTEER reportedly carries a .38 caliber revolver in his car when travelling.

M. Associates

Chief WILLIAM R. ELLIOTT, Quitman, Georgia, Police Department, advised MILTEER is well known to all persons in Quitman. MILTEER is considered eccentric and has no close associates in this city.

MILTEER is closely associated with a known prostitute, Mrs. C. C. COFIELD, 212 South Troupe Street, Valdosta, Georgia, and spends a great deal of his time at the above address.

II. CONNECTIONS WITH HATE-TYPE ORGANIZATIONS

Confidential Informant AT T-1, on May 18, 1962, made available to Atlanta a leaflet captioned "The Last Days of the Republic, Urgent Call to All White Christian Voters in Georgia" signed "G. Seals Aiken, Chairman and Founder, Constitution Party of Georgia, 1104-5 First National Bank Building, Atlanta, Georgia" and "J. A. (JOE) MILTEER, Organization Director, Constitution Party of Georgia, Quitman, Georgia."

- 6 -

Documents

AT 157-608

This pamphlet urged persons to attend a meeting at the Red
Barn, Highway 80, Macon, Georgia, on May 20, 1962. It urged
"White Christians, Believing in White Supremacy, Believing
Communism Is the Work of the Anti-Christian, and Believing It
Is Entirely Up to White Christians to Recapture Control Of
Our State and Return to Solvency" to attend and organize a
"White Christian American Grass Roots Movement."

AT T-1, on July 17, 1962, advised the above
meeting was attended by approximately fifteen unidentified
persons from Quitman, Georgia. Approximately eight persons
from Macon, Georgia, attended. The meeting was a flop.
RALPH LINDSEY, Organizer, White Citizens Council for the
Betterment of America, Macon, Georgia, sent word to this
meeting of the Constitution Party that the people of Macon
were organized and that this party was not necessary and
was not wanted in Macon.

Chief WILLIAM R. ELLIOTT, Quitman, Georgia, Police
Department, on September 24, 1962, advised he has been
acquainted with MILTEER for approximately ten years. He
described MILTEER as being an "agitator" who spends his time
finding fault with the administration of the City of Quitman.
MILTEER makes a big to-do about his criticism and prints a
leaflet which he distributes among the residents of Quitman.
MILTEER has no close associates and Chief ELLIOTT has never
known him to meet with any group of people. His father and
mother are dead and he has no relatives in this area. He
lives alone in a large run-down house and is considered
eccentric.

MILTEER is considered to be well off financially
although he is very frugal in his living habits. He generally
drives a foreign made automobile and visits Jacksonville,
Florida, frequently. During city elections in Quitman MILTEER
talks about a third party but very few people pay any attention
to him. MILTEER has been defeated on several occasions in his
efforts to become a City Commissioner in Quitman.

Confidential Informant AT T-2, on October 11, 1963,
advised MILTEER visited Miami, Florida, on October 10, 1963,
distributing the following leaflets:

- 7 -

AT 157-608

End of Kennedy, King, Khrushchev Dictatorship;
Operation Survival; David Goes Forth to Meet Goliath; Why?;
Defender or Defector; Liars and Easter; War Time Emergencies;
Is Term "Cold War" A Lie?; and When They Take Over.

The above leaflets were critical of the United
States Supreme Court and of the Government of the United
States. They criticized the liberal element in the United
States and championed the "Right Wing" conservatism.

AT T-2 advised MILTEER was distributing the above
pamphlets to a number of trusted people throughout the United
States in an attempt to have them participate in a meeting
to be held at the Marott Hotel, Indianapolis, Indiana, on
October 19 - 20, 1963, to formulate plans to put an end to
the Kennedy, King and Khrushchev Dictatorship over the nation.
At this meeting a Board of Directors was to be picked to
supervise and direct an "underground Army" in their respective
areas. MILTEER stated "next year there is to be a lot of
killing and it may be necessary to go right into the State
Department and place several of the traitors (not identified
by MILTEER) under citizen's arrest. If these traitors resist,
they will kill them right on the spot." The above was the
purpose for forming the "Underground Army."

MILTEER described MILLER GRUBBS, Louisville,
Kentucky, as being a leader of the Constitution Party of the
United States. T-2 identified GRUBBS as being a constitutional
lawyer who also heads an organization believed to be "Citizens
For Arrest of Traitors."

Confidential Informant AT T-3, on October 15, 1963,
advised the Constitution Party of the United States would hold
a national committee meeting at the Marott Hotel, Indianapolis,
Indiana, from October 19 - 21, 1963. Dr. ARTHUR G. BLAZEY,
Indiana state chairman of the Constitution Party of the United
States was quoted in the Indianapolis Star as stating the party
was organized in Indianapolis in 1960 to "correlate the efforts
of conservative votes in all states who have finally realized
that we have been denied a two party system for the past thirty
years." Lieutenant General Padro A. del Valle, United States
Marine Corps (Retired), Annapolis, Maryland, was to be the main
speaker. Dr. BLAZEY described General del Valle as being one
who has not retired from the battle to serve this country from

- 8 -

AT 157-608

such enemies as the United Nations and current administration collaborators who want to strip our Republic of all defense arms and resources in order to subject our people to one-world tyranny.

Confidential Informant AT T-2, on October 30, 1963, advised that on the evening of October 18, 1963, approximately thirty individuals met at the Marott Hotel in Indianapolis, Indiana. KENNETH GOFF from Colorado, who reportedly heads a group known as "Soldiers of the Cross" spoke against KENNEDY, the Government, and said that the Government is full of Communists and indicated he was not satisfied with the Constitution Party of the United States. MILTEER spoke along the same lines as GOFF and suggested having a hard core group formed to prevent the United States Government from being taken over by Communists.

On October 18, 1962, MILTEER, LEE McCLOUD, EARL LINDER and WILLIAM SOMERSETT met in Room 222 of the Marott Hotel. The purpose of this meeting was to discuss and take appropriate action to prevent JAMES VENABLE, Klansman from Atlanta, Georgia, from addressing the Constitution Party of the United States. It was believed that VENABLE would be identified with the Ku Klux Klan and that this would go against their choice for President, Senator STROM THURMAN.

Confidential Informant AT T-4, on November 4, 1963, advised that on October 18 - 20, 1963, MILTEER and LEE McCLOUD roomed together in Room 220, Marott Hotel, Indianapolis, Indiana. Both were attending the convention of the Constitution Party of the United States. From a conversation between MILTEER and McCLOUD, T-4 learned that McCLOUD admired JACK BROWN, Chattanooga, Tennessee. McCLOUD described BROWN as being a Klansman, and stated that he admired him more than any Klansman he had ever met. T-4 was of the opinion that McCLOUD met BROWN while en route to Indianapolis.

T-4 advised that McCLOUD stated the United States Government was spending $10,000 monthly protecting someone in his neighborhood in Atlanta, Georgia. This person had been visited by MARTIN LUTHER KING and GUS HALL. MILTEER commented that he could kill this individual by Tuesday. MILTEER did not relish killing but he could do it. MILTEER stated he would first have to see this individual so that he would not kill the wrong man. T-4 learned that this individual was (First Name Unknown) COLE, head of the Student Non-Violent Committee, Atlanta, Georgia.

- 9 -

for review at FBIHQ by
HSC-A Committee
LITTLE 5/20/77
R. Somerset

187

AT 157-608

JAMES FORMAN, Executive Secretary, Student Non-Violent
Coordinating Committee, on October 25, 1963, advised that there
is no one named COLE employed by the Student Non-Violent Coordinating
Committee. COLE could possibly be identical with EARL JULIUS COLE,
Negro male student of Morehouse College, Atlanta.

Chief WILLIAM R. ELLIOTT, Quitman, Georgia, Police
Department, on October 25, 1963, advised the Student Non-Violent
Coordinating Committee has not been active in the Quitman area.
He knew of no one named COLE in this area that could be the object
of MILTEER's threat.

T-4 advised MILTEER claimed he ran for Governor of
Georgia under the Constitution Party of Georgia. MILTEER also
claimed he was the Regional Director of the southeastern states
of the Constitution Party of the United States.

On October 20, 1963, MILTEER was advised by the
national committee of the Constitution Party that he was not
entitled to use the above designation since such a title did
not exist in the party. MILTEER was advised that AIKENS was
the chairman of the Constitution Party of Georgia. MILTEER
claimed that AIKENS was not active. MILTEER was then advised
to contact AIKENS and work it out with him to get himself
elected to the National Committee by the Georgia delegation.
After MILTEER left the closed session of the National Committee
it was indicated that the members of this committee did not
trust MILTEER.

T-4 learned that MILTEER and WALLACE BUTTERWORTH were
enemies and that MILTEER indicated that BUTTERWORTH was to be
eliminated when the time comes.

It has been ascertained that HERBERT W. BUTTERWORTH
is an officer in the National Knights of the Ku Klux Klan
and is Secretary of the Defensive Legion of Registered
Americans, Inc., which is described as an anti-Semitic and
anti-Negro organization.

An article entitled "Constitutionists Develop Split"
appeared in the October 23, 1963, edition of the "Indianapolis
Star", Indianapolis, Indiana. This article quoted CURTIS B. DALL,

- 10 -

AT 157-608

Curtis Dall

National Chairman, Constitution Party of the United States, as
stating that several hundred representatives at the above meeting
indicated that they would prefer United States Senator BARRY M.
GOLDWATER for their Presidential nominee. A movement against
STROM THURMOND appeared when the National Committee started a move
to kick out J. A. MILTEER, Quitman, Georgia, for declaring himself Regional Chairman for THURMOND in the Southeastern states.
MILTEER had driven a truck plastered with signs advocating the
nomination of THURMOND from Georgia. He spoke freely to the
press. This rankled Colonel DALL, who considers himself spokes-
man.

       After the threat to expel MILTEER from the party, an
executive committee was held. This committee meeting was
attended by MILTEER. At the conclusion of the meeting MILTEER
said that DALL and the Executive Committee informed him that he
could stay within party ranks but he would have to confine his
activity to the State of Georgia. T-4 said that MILTEER was
dejected and disgusted with the above meeting of the Constitution
Party of the United States.

       Confidential Informant T-2, on November 9, 1963,
advised that MILTEER visited Miami, Florida, on that date.
While in Miami, MILTEER advised that plans were in the
making to kill President JOHN F. KENNEDY at some future date.
MILTEER suggested JACK BROWN, Chattanooga, Tennessee, as the
man who could do the job and indicated that he would be willing
to help. While being questioned concerning the plan, MILTEER
stated he was familiar with Washington and the job could be
done from an office or hotel in the vicinity of the White House
by using a high powered rifle. MILTEER also advised that JACK
BROWN had made attempts to follow MARTIN LUTHER KING in an
effort to kill KING but never did get an opportunity.

       T-2, on November 12, 1963, advised MILTEER is forming
a new political party as opposed to the Republican and Democratic
Parties. MILTEER suggested that he is naming his new party the
"American Constitutional Party" or a name similar to this. This
organization will be composed of a hard core underground whose
identity will be secret. KENNETH ADAMS, Anniston, Alabama, and
JACK BROWN, Chattanooga, Tennessee, are to be invited to join
as underground members. The organization will be used as a
front and the only individual to be exposed will be MILTEER.

- 11 -

189

AT 157-608

T-2, on November 14, 1963, made available the principles and objectives of the Constitutional American Parties of the United States as furnished by MILTEER:

"PRINCIPLES AND OBJECTIVES OF THE CONSTITUTIONAL AMERICAN PARTIES (C A P) OF THE UNITED STATES.

"1.   Uphold and defend the United States Constitution and State Rights.

2.   Keep State and Church separate; Uphold right of Prayer and reading of the Holy Bible in Public Schools.

3.   Demand and support a strong, well trained, armed National Armed Forces commanded by tried and proven real, red-blooded, dedicated, patriotic Americans.

4.   Restore and enforce The Monroe Doctrine.

5.   Uphold and defend individuals' rights to have and bear arms to protect their homes, (their castles).

6.   Uphold and support Free Enterprise, - (Right to work Law).

7.   Protect business in whom it may hire and fire, serve and not serve.

8.   Stop Foreign Aid to all Communist Countries and their Satellites.

9.   Return control of our money to Congress.

10. Cut Federal spending and reduce taxes, balance the budget.

11. Limit powers of United States Supreme Court to decisions only.

- 12 -

190

AT 157-608

12. Limit Executive Powers of the President.

13. Seek out and remove any and all Traitors in
every branch of the Federal Government where-
ever found.

14. Defend and support individuals' right to vote
for Free Electors.

15. Work for and urge all Americans to register
and vote.

16. Get the United States out of the United Nations
and get the United Nations out of the United
States.

For more detailed information write and send
donations to

J. A. Milteer, National Chairman,

Constitutional American Parties,
(C A P), (The Constructive Parties)

P. O. Box 873

Valdosta, Ga."

T-2 on November 26, 1963, advised MILTEER departed
from Jacksonville, Florida, on November 23, 1963, by automobile
en route to Columbia, South Carolina. During this trip MILTEER
stated he had been in Houston, Fort Worth and Dallas, Texas,
as well as New Orleans, Louisiana, Biloxi and Jackson,
Mississippi, and Tuscaloosa, Alabama. MILTEER said he was
acquainted with R. E. DAVIS, Dallas, Texas, whom he described
as a "good man." He did not indicate on what days he was in
the above cities except for Tuscaloosa, Alabama.

While in Tuscaloosa, Alabama, MILTEER contacted
ROBERT SHELTON, United Klans of America, Inc., Knights of the
Ku Klux Klan, on the evening prior to the bombing of the
Sixteenth Street Baptist Church, Birmingham, Alabama, on
September 15, 1963. MILTEER described SHELTON as being against
violence and stated he was not dependable.

- 13 -

AT 157-608

MILTEER stated that MARTIN LUTHER KING and Attorney
General ROBERT KENNEDY are now unimportant. He stated their
next move would be against "Big Jew" noting that there is a
Communist conspiracy by the Jews to overthrow the United States
Government.

T-2 advised on the morning of November 24, 1963,
while at the Wade-Hampton Hotel, Columbia, South Carolina,
MILTEER stated that they did not have worry about LEE HARVEY
OSWALD getting caught because he "doesn't know anything" and
that the "right wing" is in the clear. MILTEER stated "The
patriots have outsmarted the Communists and had infiltrated
the Communist group in order that they could carry out the plan
without the right wingers becoming involved."

T-2, on November 26, 1963, advised MILTEER, on
November 24, 1963, held a meeting in the Wade-Hampton Hotel,
Columbia, South Carolina. Attending this meeting were
BELTON MIMS and A. C. BOLEN, members of the Association
for South Carolina Klans. JACK HENDRICKS, Denmark, South
Carolina, and WILL ULMER, Orangeburg, South Carolina, also
attended. MILTEER discussed the Principles and Objectives
of the Constitutional American Parties of the United States.
Prior to the arrival of the above persons MILTEER made notes
on hotel stationery captioned, "Notice to All Christians."
On these notes MILTEER stated "The Zionist Jews killed Christ
two thousand years ago and on November 22, 1963, they killed
President KENNEDY. You Jews killed the President. We are
going to kill you." The note was signed "International
Underground."

MILTEER advised the above persons that he was
preparing a pamphlet which he wanted to disseminate throughout
the country. In view of the recent events in Dallas, Texas,
he would have to alter the information he was setting out in
his pamphlet.

BELTON MIMS, in a private conversation with T-2,
questioned T-2 indicating that he was not too familiar with
MILTEER's activities.

FD-302 (Rev. 1-25-60)

FEDERAL BUREAU OF INVESTIGATION

Date ___December 1, 1963___

JOSEPH ADAMS MILTEER, Quitman, Georgia, was
interviewed November 27, 1963, at which time he advised
that during April, 1963, he attended a national meeting
of the Congress of Freedom, New Orleans, Louisiana. He
described this organization as one that believed in
Americanism and he attended this meeting as the result
of an invitation by a Mr. THOMAS, Chairman of the organization, Omaha, Nebraska. He stated during this meeting
neither he nor anyone in his presence discussed the
assassination of President KENNEDY.

MILTEER stated further that in June, 1963, he
went to Dallas, Texas, to attempt to persuade DAN SMOOT,
author of the "Dan Smoot Report" to run as Vice-President
on the Constitution Party ticket in the election in
November, 1964. He stated he had no other business in
Dallas.

MILTEER further stated that on October 18-20,
1963, he traveled to Indianapolis, Indiana, with BILL
SOMERSETT of Miami, Florida, and LEE McCLOUD of Atlanta,
Georgia. They attended the National Convention of the
Constitution Party. He stated he attended this meeting
as the result of an invitation by CURTIS B. DALL, former
son-in-law of the late President FRANKLIN D. ROOSEVELT.

MILTEER described himself as a non-dues-paying
member of the White Citizens Council of Atlanta, Georgia,
the Congress of Freedom and the Constitution Party.

MILTEER emphatically denies ever making threats
to assassinate President KENNEDY or participating in any
such assassination. He stated he has never heard anyone
make such threats. He also denied making threats against
anyone subsequent to the assassination of Presidnet KENNEDY.
He stated he does not know, nor has he ever been in the
presence of LEE HARVEY OSWALD or JACK RUBY to his knowledge.

MILTEER denied any knowledge of the bombing of
the Sixteenth Street Baptist Church in Birmingham, Alabama,
on September 15, 1963.

- 15 -

On __11/27/63__ at __Quitman, Georgia__   File # _____

SAs KENNETH A. WILLIAMS and
by __DONALD A. ADAMS__   :cb/saa   Date dictated __12/1/63__

This document contains neither recommendations nor conclusions of the FBI. It is the property of the FBI and is loaned to
your agency; it and its contents are not to be distributed outside your agency.

AT 157-608

     T-2, on December 1, 1963, advised he met with BELTON MIMS and A. O. BOLEN of the Association for South Carolina Klans at Columbia, South Carolina, on November 28, 1963. They discussed the assassination of President KENNEDY, the Constitutional American Parties of the United States and MILTEER. MIMS and BOLEN expressed their regrets over the assassination of President KENNEDY and questioned T-2 as to whether MILTEER could have been involved. MIMS was concerned over a statement made by MILTEER that the "Right Wing" had nothing to worry about. MIMS questioned T-2 concerning the relationship between MILTEER, JACK BROWN, Chattanooga, Tennessee, KENNETH ADAMS, Anniston, Alabama, and BOB SHELTON, Tuscaloosa, Alabama. MIMS was concerned as to whether MILTEER had actually formed an underground group unknown to the Klan. MILTEER and BOLAN both stated they had agreed to join with MILTEER in a campaign to blame President KENNEDY's death on the Jews. They also indicated that they would assist MILTEER in forming the Constitutional American Parties of the United States.

     T-2, on December 1, 1963, made available the following pamphlet which was prepared by MILTEER:

"WAKE UP - - CHRISTIANS"

"The Jews had Jesus killed nearly 2000 years ago. They have not changed in all this time. They, the Zionist Jews, Communists, had President JOHN FITZGERALD KENNEDY killed in Dallas, Texas, by LEE OSWALD, November 22, 1963. LEE OSWALD, in turn, was killed by JACK RUBINSTEIN. All violence committed by left wing groups.

"It now becomes the solemn duty of every true, red-blooded American to seek, find, expel, drive out from our country every traitor be he a Zionist Jew, Communist, or what have you.

"Give us liberty or we'll give you death.

"International Underground"

- 16 -

Documents

AT   157-608

      T-2, on December 10, 1963, furnished the following
letter, which was mailed from Valdosta, Georgia, on December
9, 1963, from MILTEER:

           "CONSTITUTIONAL AMERICAN PARTIES OF U. S.
           Post Office Box 873
           Valdosta, Georgia
           J. A. Milteer, National Chairman

               "Dec. 9, 1963.

      "Due to recent events which have taken place
within our American borders that may, in time,
change the course of history, and the usual holidays
before us, it is deemed advisable to curtail any
contemplated meetings of our Constitutional American
Parties of the United States movement until early
in the new year of 1964. You will be advised of
any meeting which may be called for early in
January, 1964.

      "Since we are 'Right Wing' and it is our
aim and intention to uphold and defend our United
States Constitution against all enemies, both
within and without our borders, we may be called
before the F. B. I. for questioning relative to
many things. You are advised to cooperate fully
but do so on your Constitutional American Parties
rights. Do not go alone for any conference or to
answer any questions to any F. B. I. office. Be
interviewed in your own home or office with some one
present or with others present with you. Do not at
any time be interviewed alone with any F. B. I. Agent
or Agents.

      "If a telephone call comes to you any where,
your home, office or any other place requesting you
to meet with some one at any certain place, street
corner, building, home, business place, church,
synagogue or any where, wait a few minutes and call
the person who called you to arrange any such meeting
to see if it is authentic and for further detailed
instructions. This will verify the call and make it

- 17 -

195

AT 157-608

clear in your mind whether it is a frame-up or not.
Then to further keep yourself in the clear, remain
in your home or business place, do not go any where
and do not meet with anybody. Frame-ups to involve
any and all 'Right Wing' followers may be in the
making by none other than the F. B. I. Be very
cautious.

"I extend to you and your family a warm, hearty
and Merry Christmas, followed with a Happy, Prosperous
New Year with blessings from our LORD and SAVIOUR
JESUS CHRIST throughout the entire 1964 year.

"Yours for the return to GOD ALMIGHTY, the BIBLE
and our United States Constitution in 1964.

"/s/ J. A. Milteer."

Confidential Informant AT T-5, on December 4,
1963, advised he is acquainted with BELTON MIMS and A. O.
BOLEN, members of the Association of South Carolina Klans,
and WILL ULMER, Orangeburg, South Carolina. T-5 could
furnish no information regarding any meeting of members
of the Association of South Carolina Klans held at the Wade-
Hampton Hotel, Columbia, South Carolina, on November 24,
1963. MIMS and BOLEN are members of Klavern 335, Association
of South Carolina Klans, West Columbia, South Carolina.
~~~~~~~~~ have never given indication of advocating violence in
connection with the racial issue. T-5 advised there is no
group known as the Constitutional American Parties of the
United States at Columbia, South Carolina.

III.   STATEMENTS MADE BY SUBJECT CONCERNING VIOLENCE
        AND ACTIVITY IN RACIAL SITUATIONS.

Confidential Informant AT T-2, on October 11,
1963, advised MILTEER was in Miami, Florida, on October
10, 1963, distributing leaflets urging people to attend a
meeting of the Constitution Party of the United States at
Indianapolis, Indiana, on October 19 - 20, 1963. At this
meeting MILTEER claimed that a Board of Directors was to be
picked to supervise an "Underground Army." MILTEER stated

- 18 -

Documents

AT 157-608

"next year there is to be a lot of killing and it may even be
necessary to go right into the State Department and place
some of the Traitors, not identified by MILTEER, under citizens
arrest. If these traitors resist, they will kill them right
on the spot."

Confidential Informant AT T-4, on November 4, 1964,
advised MILTEER, on October 18 - 20, 1963, attended the
convention of the Constitution Party of the United States
held at the Marott Hotel, Indianapolis, Indiana. MILTEER
roomed with LEE McCLOUD in Room 220 of the above hotel.
McCLOUD, in a conversation with MILTEER, stated the United
States Government was spending $10,000 monthly protecting
someone in his neighborhood in Atlanta. This individual had
been visited by MARTIN LUTHER KING and GUS HALL. MILTEER
commented that he could kill this individual by Tuesday. He
did not relish killing but he could do it. He would first
have to see this individual so that he would not kill the
wrong man. The individual referred to was (First Name
Unknown) COLE, head of the Student Nonviolent Committee,
Atlanta, Georgia.

JAMES FORMAN, Executive Secretary, Student Nonviolent
Coordinating Committee, on October 25, 1963, advised that there
is no one named COLE employed by the Student Nonviolent
Coordinating Committee. COLE could possibly be identical
with EARL JULIUS COLE, Negro male student at Morehouse College,
Atlanta.

Chief WILLIAM R. ELLIOTT, Quitman, Georgia, Police
Department, on October 25, 1963, advised the Student Nonviolent
Coordinating Committee has not been active in the Quitman,
Georgia, area. He knew of no one named COLE in this area
that could be the object of MILTEER's threat.

Confidential Informant AT T-2, on November 9,
1963, advised MILTEER was visiting in Miami, Florida, on
that date. MILTEER talked about plans in the making to
kill President KENNEDY at some future date. He suggested
JACK BROWN, Chattanooga, Tennessee, as being the man who
could do the job and indicated that he would be willing to
help. MILTEER stated he was familiar with Washington and
the job could be done from an office or hotel in the vicinity
of the White House by using a high powered rifle.

- 19 -

AT 157-608

T-2, on November 20, 1963, advised that MILTEER, on November 9, 1963, told him that he was forming a new political party as opposed to the Republican and Democratic Parties. This Constitutional American Parties of the United States was to be comprised of a hard core underground whose identity will be secret. KENNETH ADAMS, Anniston, Alabama, and JACK BROWN, Chattanooga, Tennessee, are to be invited to join as underground members. The organization is to be used as a front and the only individual to be exposed will be MILTEER.

T-2, on November 26, 1963, advised that MILTEER was in the Union Train Station, Jacksonville, Florida, on November 23, 1963. MILTEER stated he was very jubilate over the death of President KENNEDY. MILTEER stated "Everything ran true to form. I guess you thought I was kidding you when I said he would be killed from a window with a high powered rifle."

When questioned as to whether he was guessing when he originally made the threat regarding the President, MILTEER stated, "I don't do any guessing."

- 20 -

APPENDIX

NATIONAL KU KLUX KLAN, also known as
Knights of the Ku Klux Klan, Inc.,
National Grand Council of the Knights
of the Ku Klux Klan, National Knights
of the Ku Klux Klan, Majority Citizens
League

A source advised that on May 22, 1960, the National
Grand Council of the Knights of the Ku Klux Klan met at
Atlanta, Georgia, to discuss consolidation of the klans
unity of effort and activities, to establish a National Fund
and a National Secretary and to design a new flag. The
meeting was attended by representatives of the Federation
of Ku Klux Klan, Alabama; Association of Arkansas Klans,
Arkansas; Florida Knights of the Ku Klux Klan, Florida;
Southern Knights of the Ku Klux Klan, Florida; Association
of Georgia Klans, Georgia; Knights of the Ku Klux Klan,
North Carolina; Association of South Carolina Klans, South
Carolina; Dixie Knights of the Ku Klux Klan, Tennessee;
and Hyksos Klan, Texas.

This source advised that at a consolidation meeting at
Atlanta, Georgia, September 2-5, 1960, at which the North
Carolina and Texas Klans were not represented, it was resolved
and passed that their name be changed to National Ku Klux
Klan.

This source also advised that at a consolidation meeting
at Savannah, Georgia, October 3, 1960, it was resolved and
passed that in any future meetings of this group the name
"Majority Citizens League" was to be used.

A second source advised that at a national klonklave
meeting at Texarkana, Texas, on February 11-12, 1961, a motion
was carried that there were to be at least six national
meetings a year to be held any time from one week to twelve
weeks after the last meeting. The time and meeting place were
to be decided by the newly elected chairman. This second
source also advised that at each meeting a new chairman and
acting secretary were to be elected to serve at the next
meeting. A national secretary had not been appointed.

APPENDIX

- 20a -

APPENDIX

ASSOCIATION OF SOUTH CAROLINA KLANS
KNIGHTS OF THE KU KLUX KLAN (ASCK)

A source advised on September 24, 1956, that the
Association of South Carolina Klans (ASCK) was organized
in the Fall of 1955 and is patterned after the Association
of Carolina Klans (ACK). This source said ASCK is a new
organization and not a rebirth of ACK, although all high-
ranking officials of ASCK had been members of ACK. The
source stated announced purposes of this organization are
to promote white supremacy and combat integration of the
races; however, the use of violence is disavowed.

A second source advised on September 2, 1950, that
ACK was composed of groups formerly members of the Association
of Georgia Klans (AGK) and although ACK severed all connections
with AGK on November 14, 1959, the ideals, purposes and policies
of the two organizations remained identical. ACK became defunct
after conviction and imprisonment of its highest official and
other members in 1952.

A third source advised on September 16, 1962, that
ASCK continues to operate for the purpose of promoting white
supremacy and combating integration by peaceful means by
public speaking and propaganda.

This third source said that ASCK, using the name
Majority Citizens League of South Carolina, published a
monthly newspaper, "Southland Standard," from August through
December, 1961, and dropped it due to lack of financial support.

AGK has been designated by the Attorney General
pursuant to Executive Order 10450.

APPENDIX

- 21 -

APPENDIX

UNITED KLANS OF AMERICA, INC.
KNIGHTS OF THE KU KLUX KLAN (UNITED KLANS)

Records of Superior Court of Fulton County, Georgia, show that this Klan organization was granted a corporate charter on February 21, 1961, at Atlanta, Georgia, under the name United Klans, Knights of the Ku Klux Klan of America, Inc.

A source advised on February 27, 1961, that United Klans was formed as a result of a split in U. S. Klans, Knights of the Ku Klux Klan, Inc. According to the source, the split resulted from a leadership dispute and United Klans has the same aims and objectives as the parent group. These are the promotion of Americanism, white supremacy and segregation of the races.

The first source and a second source advised in July, 1961, that United Klans, Knights of the Ku Klux Klan of America, Inc., merged with Alabama Knights, Knights of the Ku Klux Klan. The merged organization established headquarters in Suite 401, The Alston Building, Tuscaloosa, Alabama. The organization is directed by ROBERT SHELTON, Imperial Wizard, and is the dominant Klan group in the South with units in several southern states.

On August 14, 1963, the second source advised that the organization formerly known as United Klans, Knights of the Ku Klux Klan of America, Inc., would be known in the future as United Klans of America, Inc., Knights of the Ku Klux Klan. The second source said the name was changed by a resolution adopted at the National Klonvocation held July 8, 1961, at Indian Springs, Georgia.

Second source advised that at a meeting of Prattville, Alabama, on October 22, 1961, a majority of the Klaverns of the U. S. Klans, Knights of the Ku Klux Klan merged with the United Klans of America, Inc., Knights of the Ku Klux Klan.

APPENDIX

— 22* —

FD-204 (Rev. 3-3-59)

UNITED STATES DEPARTMENT OF JUSTICE
FEDERAL BUREAU OF INVESTIGATION

Copy to:

Report of:	SA CHARLES S. HARDING	Office:	Atlanta, Georgia
Date:	December 1, 1963		
Field Office File #:	105-3193	Bureau File #:	
Title:	LEE HARVEY OSWALD		

Character: INTERNAL SECURITY - R

Synopsis:

Miss VEREEN ALEXANDER, Thomasville, Ga., stated LEE HARVEY OSWALD possibly present at a party summer of 1963 in New Orleans, La., which was attended by individuals who formerly discussed how one would go about the assassination of the President. Mr. and Mrs. STEVE ALLEN BRILL in Mexico, September, 1963, but did not see anyone resembling OSWALD on trips to Mexico. Mr. and Mrs. ROBERT HOWARD PEAVY and Chief of Police HERBERT JENKINS and Mrs. JENKINS in Mexico, September, 1963, and did not see anyone who resembled OSWALD. Informant reports racketeer named RUBIN formerly lived in Daytona, Fla., and pictures of JACK LEON RUBY appear similar to RUBIN. JOHN O'LEARY of theatrical agency, and ANDY MARINOS, manager of Domino Lounge, Atlanta, both in contact with RUBY over past several years in connection with booking acts into RUBY's night club. AT T-2 advised believed RUBY active in arranging illegal flights of weapons from Miami to Castro organization in Cuba in 1950's. RUBY also allegedly purchased substantial share in Havana gaming house. MARION HAYES, long distance telephone operator, Atlanta, advised approximately three weeks previous to assassination of President on Sunday, she was requested to place calls by same person to LEE HARVEY OSWALD in New Orleans and Dallas and JACK RUBENSTEIN in Dallas. She was finally able to get both calls through. Admitted she has been emotionally upset concerning the assassination of

The next six pages (pp. 202-207) are excerpts from the 33-page December 1, 1963 Harding report that show its nature, an odd collection of strange accusations concerning the assassination. Even though there are only four pages about him, this becomes the document for official research into Milteer. (Continued next page→)

AT 105-3193

President KENNEDY and was watching television at the time
RUBY shot OSWALD and noticed just prior to the shooting that
OSWALD appeared to recognize RUBY. Unknown individual
allegedly called office of Governor CARL SANDERS of Georgia
and made an implied threat to receptionist. JAMES WOLLWEBER,
private pilot, stated an individual named JOHNSON called
him from Miami and wanted him to pick up an unknown individual
in Dallas, Tex., on 11/23/63 and fly him to Nassau. WOLLWEBER
unable to make trip because of bad weather. CHARLES BASCOM
WEATHERLY, Atlanta, Ga., admitted calling the U. S. Supreme
Court while in an intoxicated condition and accused Chief
Justice WARREN and Associate Justice BLACK of being responsible for the death of the President. JOSEPH ADAMS MILTEER
Quitman, Ga., advised that he was in New Orleans in April
of 1963 and in Dallas, Tex., in June of 1963 in connection
with his activity in patriotic organizations. Denied any
knowledge of assassination of President KENNEDY and denied
making any threats that he would assassinate the President.
JOE CUMMING, correspondent, "Newsweek" magazine, did not
witness shooting of OSWALD by RUBY. HAL SUIT advised received
from source OSWALD in Atlanta August or September, 1963,
following announcement President KENNEDY was going to speak
at Georgia Tech. Allegedly stayed at Holiday Inn and had
gun. Individuals employed at Holiday Inn interviewed and
some believe individual could possibly be OSWALD but others
believe individual was not OSWALD.

-P-

DETAILS:

- 2 -

The Warren Commission completely ignores Milteer. Later in 1976, when the House
Select Committee on Assassinations actually looked into the Milteer accusations,
the Harding report's statement of his height as 5'4" carried much of the weight in
invalidating his presence at Dealey Plaza on November 22, 1963.

FD-302 (Rev. 1-25-60)

FEDERAL BUREAU OF INVESTIGATION

Date ___December 1, 1963___

1

        AT T-2 advised on November 29, 1963, that he
formerly owned interest in a club in Miami, Florida. He
stated that in the early 1950's, JACK RUBY held interest
in the Colonial Inn, a nightclub and gambling house in
Hollandale, Florida. He stated that JACK RUBY, known then
as RUBENSTEIN, was active in arranging illegal flights of
weapons from Miami to the Castro organization in Cuba.
According to T-2, RUBY was reportedly part owner of two
planes used for these purposes.

        T-2 further stated that RUBY subsequently left
Miami and purchased a substantial share in a Havana gaming
house in which one COLLIS PRIO (phonetic) was principal
owner. T-2 stated that COLLIS PRIO was within favor of
former Cuban leader BATISTA, but was instrumental in
financing and managing accumulation of arms by pro-Castro
forces.

        T-2 stated that one DONALD EDWARD BROWDER was
associated with RUBY in the arms smuggling operation.
BROWDER is reportedly incarcerated in the U. S. Penitentiary,
Atlanta, after conviction on a U. S. Customs violation.
T-2 also stated that JOE MARRS of Marrs Aircraft, 167th
Street, Miami, Florida, allegedly contracted with RUBY to
make flights to Havana. T-2 further stated that LESLIE LEWIS,
formerly Chief of Police, Hialeah, Florida, and now possibly
a pistol instructor in Dade County, Florida, Sheriff's Office,
possessed detailed knowledge of persons involved in flight
of weapons to Cuba and had specific knowledge of RUBY's
participation.

        T-2 subsequently advised on November 30, 1963,
that on the basis of viewing RUBY's photograph and knowing
that the JACK RUBENSTEIN he has described originally resided
in Chicago, Illinois, he is convinced beyond reasonable
doubt that the latter is identical with the JACK RUBY in
Dallas, Texas. T-2 also named CLIFTON T. BOWES, Jr.,
formerly captain of National Airlines, Miami, Florida, as

- 14 -

On __11/29/63 &__
__11/30/63__ at __Atlanta, Georgia__   File # __Atlanta 105-3193__

by ____SA DANIEL D. DOYLE :cb____   Date dictated __12/1/63__

This document contains neither recommendations nor conclusions of the FBI. It is the property of the FBI and is loaned to
your agency; it and its contents are not to be distributed outside your agency.

Documents

AT 105-3193
2

having been acquainted with RUBENSTEIN and his activities.
At this time T-2 added that DONALD EDWARD BROWDER was also
formerly active in the illegal liquor market.

AT 105-193
CSH:cb
1

On November 30, 1963, Warden D. M. HERITAGE,
U. S. Penitentiary, Atlanta, Georgia, advised that a check
of the records of the U. S. Penitentiary failed to reflect
a person by the name of DONALD EDWARD BROWDER as ever being
an inmate at the U. S. Penitentiary. Records reflect that
one EDDIE BROWDER was formerly incarcerated on a liquor
violation and was released in 1960.

AT 105-3193
CSH/evg/hld
1

On November 23, 1963, Washington Field Office
advised that advice had been received from police officials
at the United States Supreme Court on that date that they had
received a telephone call on the evening of November 22, 1963,
from a man who identified himself as C. D. or C. B. WEATHERLY,
2374-A Lindmont Circle, Atlanta, Georgia, who was allegedly
employed by the Studebaker Company, 910 Rhodes-Haverty Building,
Atlanta.

In this call WEATHERLY stated that Chief Justice
WARREN and Associate Justice BLACK were "responsible for the
death of the President." WEATHERLY wanted to be contacted by
the Supreme Court police or the FBI and stated "If the FBI
did not contact him, he would take other measures."

FD-302 (Rev. 1-25-60)   FEDERAL BUREAU OF INVESTIGATION

1   Date November 26, 1963

CHARLES BASCOM WEATHERLY, 2374-A Lindmont Circle,
N. E., advised he is employed as Regional Marketing Analyst
for the Studebaker Automotive Sales Corporation, Atlanta,
Georgia.

He stated that he had become upset over the assassination of President KENNEDY and made a telephone call to the
United States Supreme Court while in an intoxicated condition.

WEATHERLY stated that he had no information concerning
Chief Justice WARREN or Associate Justice BLACK being responsible
for the death of the President and had no information that he
could furnish to the FBI. Concerning "other measures" he would
take if not contacted by the FBI, WEATHERLY stated that he
had nothing specific in mind and attributed all of his statements
to his intoxicated condition.

FD-302 (Rev. 1-25-60)

FEDERAL BUREAU OF INVESTIGATION

Date _____12-1-63_____

1

        MARION HAYES, long distance telephone operator, Southern Bell Telephone and Telegraph Company, Atlanta, advised that approximately three weeks before on a Sunday evening, she placed a long distance call to LEE HARVEY OSWALD at New Orleans, Louisiana, for a person using a credit card with numbers ending in S32. She stated she recalled this call was placed from the Dogwood Motel, Chamblee, Georgia. She requested the information operator in New Orleans to obtain LEE HARVEY OSWALD's telephone number and after obtaining same, she made repeated efforts to contact this number but was unsuccessful. She stated that the caller then gave her a Dallas number for OSWALD and she was unable to reach him in Dallas. The caller then had her contact the New Orleans number again but she was unsuccessful in locating OSWALD.

        Miss HAYES added that approximately 10:00 p.m. that same evening, the same person using the same credit card number requested her to call OSWALD in Dallas, Texas, at which time the call was completed.

        Miss HAYES stated further that the same caller using the same credit card number then attempted to reach JACK RUBENSTEIN at a number in Dallas, Texas. No one answered this number and the caller then asked her to contact the information operator in Dallas for the telephone number of JACK RUBENSTEIN or JACK RUBY stating everyone in Dallas would know him as he operated a night club. Miss HAYES stated that the information operator gave her a telephone number which number she called but there was no answer. She stated the caller then instructed her to call JACK RUBENSTEIN's sister, MYRTLE, in Dallas, Texas, furnishing the number and this call was completed. She stated that approximately 1:00 a.m. the following morning, this same person using the same credit card number placed a call to Dallas, Texas, for JACK RUBENSTEIN and the call was completed.

- 28 -

On ___11-26-63___ at ___Atlanta, Georgia___ File # ___AT 105-3193___

by ___SAs JACK T. BEVERSTEIN and___ :jkw Date dictated ___12-1-63___
        ALDEN F. MILLER

AT 105-3193
JTB:jkw
2

Miss HAYES stated that she has approximately twenty years' experience with the Southern Bell Telephone Company. She stated she has been emotionally upset concerning the assassination of President KENNEDY and has been watching television continuously concerning the events in Washington and Dallas. She stated she was watching television at the time RUBY shot OSWALD and she noticed just prior to RUBY shooting OSWALD that OSWALD appeared to recognize him.

FD-302 (Rev. 1-25-60)

FEDERAL BUREAU OF INVESTIGATION

Date _____12-1-63_____

1

THEODORE A. KING, State Security Officer for Southern Bell Telephone and Telegraph Company, advised that it was very improbable that the same telephone operator would have received and placed all of the calls described by MARION HAYES.

Mr. KING made available the record of cancelled calls for the dates of November 3, 10, and 17, 1963, (Sundays) and a review of these cancelled calls failed to reveal any as mentioned by Miss HAYES.

UNITED STATES DEPARTMENT OF JUSTICE

FEDERAL BUREAU OF INVESTIGATION

In Reply, Please Refer to
File No.

105-3193

Atlanta, Georgia
December 1, 1963

Title   **LEE HARVEY OSWALD**

Character   **INTERNAL SECURITY - RUSSIA**

Reference   Report of SA CHARLES S.
HARDING, December 1, 1963,
at Atlanta.

    All sources (except any listed below) whose
identities are concealed in referenced communication
have furnished reliable information in the past.

    AT T-2, who has furnished insufficient infor-
mation to determine reliability.

This letter was attached at the end of Harding's report, similar to the letter at the
end of McGraw's report [Doc. #16, p. 109] that damaged Somersett's credibility.

MM 89-35
1.

Re: THREAT TO KILL PRESIDENT KENNEDY
BY J. A. MILTEER, MIAMI, FLORIDA,
NOVEMBER 9, 1963

On November 26, 1963, a source who has furnished
reliable information in the past and in addition has
furnished some information that could not be verified or
corroborated, advised SA PETERSON as follows:

On November 23, 1963, J. A. MILTEER was in the
Union Train Station, Jacksonville, Florida, and at about
4:25 p.m. on that date stated he was very jubilant over
the death of President KENNEDY. MILTEER stated, "Everything
ran true to form. I guess you thought I was kidding you
when I said he would be killed from a window with a high-
powered rifle." When questioned as to whether he was
guessing when he originally made the threat regarding
President KENNEDY, MILTEER is quoted as saying, "I don't
do any guessing."

On the evening of November 23, 1963, MILTEER
departed Jacksonville, Florida, by automobile en route to
Columbia, South Carolina. During this trip, MILTEER
stated that he had been in Houston, Ft. Worth, and Dallas,
Texas, as well as New Orleans, Louisiana, Biloxi and
Jackson, Mississippi, and Tuscaloosa, Alabama. MILTEER
said he was acquainted with one R. E. DAVIS of Dallas,
Texas, whom he described as a "good man," but did not indicate
he was personally acquainted with DAVIS. MILTEER did not
indicate on what dates he was in the above cities, except
for Tuscaloosa, Alabama.

MILTEER related that he was in Tuscaloosa,
Alabama, and contacted ROBERT SHELTON of the United
Klans of America, Inc., Knights of the Ku Klux Klan
(United Klans), on the evening prior to the bombing of the

120

The next three pages (pp. 209-211) are the portions concerning Milteer in Robert Gemberling's initial FBI report on the JFK assassination that was used as the
basis for the Warren Commission report.

16th Street Baptist Church, Birmingham, Alabama, which
occurred on September 15, 1963. Regarding SHELTON,
MILTEER said SHELTON was against violence and could not
be depended upon.

A characterization of the United Klans of America,
Inc., Knights of the Ku Klux Klan (United Klans), follows.
Sources therein have furnished reliable information in the
past.

MILTEER related that MARTIN LUTHER KING and Attorney
General ROBERT KENNEDY are now unimportant. He stated their
next move would be against the "Big Jew" noting that there is
a communist conspiracy by the Jews to overthrow the United
States government.

MILTEER arrived in Columbia, South Carolina, about
midnight and registered at the Wade Hampton Hotel, Columbia,
South Carolina. On the morning of November 24, 1963,
MILTEER advised that they did not have to worry about LEE
HARVEY OSWALD getting caught because he "doesn't know anything"
and that the "right wing" is in the clear. MILTEER further
related that, "The patriots have outsmarted the communists
and had infiltrated the communist group in order that they
(communists) could carry out the plan without the right
wingers becoming involved."

Later, on the morning of November 24, 1963, four
individuals arrived at the Wade Hampton Hotel and conferred
with MILTEER. These individuals included BELTON MIMS and
A. O. BOLEN, members of the Association of South Carolina
Klans; JACK HENDRICKS described as a white male, 35, 5' 7",
from Denmark, South Carolina, and WILL ULMER, from
Orangeburg, South Carolina. ULMER was described as a white
male, 35, 155 pounds, yellow complexion, large eyes.

121

A characterization of the Association of South
Carolina Klans follows. Sources therein have furnished
reliable information in the past.

After their arrival, MILTEER stated that there
was no point in discussing President KENNEDY, and again
stated, "We must now concentrate on the Jews." MILTEER
advised that he was preparing a pamphlet which he wanted
to disseminate throughout the country. Prior to concluding
their discussion, information was received that JACK RUBY
had killed LEE HARVEY OSWALD. In view of this, MILTEER said
he would have to alter the information he was setting out in
his pamphlet.

The source advised that based on his contact with
MILTEER, he could not definitely state whether MILTEER was
acquainted with either RUBY or OSWALD.

Re: Threat to Kill President KENNEDY
      by J. A. MILTEER, Miami, Florida,
      November 9, 1963

J. A. MILTEER is also known as JOSEPH ADAMS MILTEER.
He was born February 26, 1902, at Quitman, Georgia, and lives
at Quitman and Valdosta, Georgia. He reportedly is a wealthy
bachelor who inherited an estimated $200,000 from his father.
He is reported to have no family, no employment and to spend a
great deal of time traveling throughout the Southeastern United
States. He has been unsuccessful in city politics in Quitman
and publishes a weekly pamphlet critizing the operation of the
Quitman City Government. MILTEER has associated himself with
the Constitution Party of the United States and attended a
convention of this party held at Indianapolis, Indiana, during
October, 1963. He was reprimanded by this party for describing himself as being the party regional chairman for the
Southeastern states. MILTEER reportedly became disillusioned
with the Constitution Party of the United States and has
attempted to form a party known as the Constitutional American
Parties of the United States. MILTEER allegedly intends to
use the Constitutional American Parties of the United States
as a front to form a hard core underground for possible violence in combatting integration.

1

DL 89-43
PEW/ds

The interview of JOSEPH ADAMS MILTEER, as well as
additional information regarding him, is contained on pages
24-26 of the report of Special Agent CHARLES S. HARDING,
Atlanta, Georgia, dated December 1, 1963, in the case
entitled "LEE HARVEY OSWALD; INTERNAL SECURITY - RUSSIA".

RELEASED PER P.L. 102
NARA _JFK_ DATE _9-13-00_

Allegation: That the FBI and/or the Secret Service
Withheld Information Relating to J. A. Milteer's
Threat to Assassinate President Kennedy.

The documentary record available to the Committee reveals
that National States Rights Party member J. A. Milteer asserted
during a November 9, 1963 conversation that President Kennedy
would be assassinated by someone using a high-powered rifle
from the window of a tall building, that Jack Brown of Chattanooga, Tennessee, was a man who might do the job and "that
afterward officers would leave no stone unturned trying to
find the killer, they will pick up someone within hours afterward just to throw the public off." This conversation was
recorded by Miami Police Department informant William Sommerset,
and verbatim transcripts were disseminated to the Secret Service
and the FBI on November 11, 1963. However, the reports provided
the Warren Commission neither recounted that the threat had
been recorded nor the specifics of the threat. Thus, the
Commission had no reason to distinguish this threat from the
hundreds of unsubstantiated allegations that poured into the
Bureau subsequent to the assassination.

On November 26, 1963, Sommerset provided additional information on Milteer, the reliability of which was established by
the tapes of a November 23, 1963 conversation. On that date,
Milteer was in the Union Train Station, Jacksonville, Florida,

TOP SECRET

The next three pages (pp. 212-214) are from the 1975 United States Senate Select Committee to Study Governmental Operations with Respect to Intelligence Activities (Church
Committee), and they show the evolution of the Milteer story, (Continued next page→)

212

RELEASED PER P.L. 102~
NARA __JFK__ DATE 9-13-00

where he stated that he was jubilant over the death of
President Kennedy, that he had stopped in Dallas on an automobile trip through southern cities, and that everything had
run true to form. Milteer further stated that:

> I guess you thought I was kidding you when I
> said he would be killed from a window with a
> high-powered rifle.

On December 1, 1963, two FBI agents interviewed Milteer
in Quitman, Georgia. According to their report:

> Milteer emphatically denied ever making threats
> to assassinate President Kennedy or partici-
> pating in such threats. He stated he has never
> heard anyone make such threats. He also denied
> ever having visited Dallas, Texas.

The Bureau documents we reviewed -- which documents we
were told represented all FBI materials gathered on Milteer
during the course of the assassination investigation -- revealed
that on the basis of Milteer's statements to the agents, and
information indicating that Milteer was in Quitman, Georgia
on November 22, 1963, the Bureau conducted no further investigation of Milteer or his known associates, one of whom was Don
Burros [whose name was found in Oswald's notebook].

The Secret Service response to the November 9, 1963,
Milteer threat is also instructive. By letter, dated January
9, 1976, the staff posed to the Secret Service certain questions
relating to Milteer and the President's November 1963 Miami and
Dallas trips. In summary, the Service acknowledged receipt of
a transcript of the tape, and the fact that further investigation

TOP SECRET

and the problem of "reading" the documents. This reports states my interview of Milteer
took place on December 1, instead of the actual date, November 27, 1963.

RELEASED PER P.L. 102~~~~ ~~~~ ~~~~
NARA JFK   DATE 9-13-00

of certain named persons associated with right wing groups
had been predicated upon receipt of the "Milteer information."
They assert that this investigation established that none of
these persons were in the Miami area on November 18, 1963.

Interestingly enough, the Secret Service response to the
question of whether Milteer's threat was considered in connection with the President's visit to Dallas on November 22, 1963,
was not that they conducted a similar investigation in Dallas
but that:

> In the absence of any information from the FBI
> to indicate any of the Milteer connected indivi-
> duals were coming to, or were present in, Dallas,
> this particular case was not considered critical.

This response is surprising in that there is no record that
the FBI was monitoring the activities of any of the named
persons on anything approaching a daily basis or that -- with
the exception of Milteer himself -- the Bureau had information
indicating that any of these persons constituted a threat to
the safety of the President, a prerequisite at that time to
the dissemination of FBI information to the Secret Service.*

TOP SECRET

---

* The record does establish that the name of one known member
of a right wing group in the Dallas area was provided to the
Secret service by the FBI. However, he was not one of the
"Milteer connected" individuals.

214

Documents

SECRET

Stenographic Transcript Of

HEARINGS

Before The

Committee on Assassinations

HOUSE OF REPRESENTATIVES

STAFF BRIEFING

E V E N I N G   S E S S I O N

Washington, D. C.

March 9, 1977

Alderson Reporting Company, Inc.

Official Reporters

300 Seventh St., S. W.   Washington, D. C.

554-2345

SECRET

The next five pages (pp. 215-219) are from the 1977 House Select Committee on Assassinations' report concerning Milteer. Interestingly, Robert Tanenbaum, HSCA counsel makes comments that the FBI should have confronted Milteer about his recorded threats, as "would be done in the ordinary course of a decent investigation."

67   SECRET   2-174

1   E. Howard Hunt was the CIA station chief in Mexico City

2   during the time the President was assassinated. This letter

3   originates from Mexico City. There has been speculation that

4   a fellow by the name of Guy Baldwin, a CIA employee, allegedly

5   had meetings in his apartment in Mexico City and therein

6   discussed plans to assassinate the President.

7   ¶ What we have to do, obviously, is inquire about the FBI

8   if they have the originals so that we could have, immediately,

9   an analysis done with the known hand of Lee Harvey Oswald and

10 compare it to this letter.

11   I do not know whether or not we will be able to do that

12 with the copies we have. Again, I would hope that that would

13 be brought up.

14   Mr. Stokes. I might say, Mr. Sprague, you should make

15 note of that for the agenda.

16   Mr. Sprague. Very well, Mr. Chairman.

17   Mr. Tanenbaum. Now, Mr. Lehner alluded to Agent 88

18 and we have heard a tape and discussed it with an individual

19 who was, at the time, a Sergeant in the Miami Police Depart-

20 ment.

21   He heard a tape on November 10, 1963 that was recorded

22 on November 9, 1963. This tape was between Mr. Somerset,

23 now deceased, and Mr. Joseph J. Milteer, who died in 1974.

24 Mr. Milteer was a rabid, right-wing activist. He went to the

25 apartment of Mr. Somerset. Mr. Somerset, in this one-room

SECRET

68

SECRET

apartment had a simple tape-recorder and tape-recorded the
conversation.

¶ In substance, what Milteer says is that the President
is going to be killed. He predicts the exact manner in
which the President is going to be killed. He says it is
going to be from an office building with a high-powered
rifle that can be disassembled, and that shortly after the
assassination the police are going to arrest someone to allay
public concern.

He does not say that the President is going to be killed
in Dallas. If anything, one can speculate about this if
one desires. It would have been in Miami, because the
President went to Miami on November 18th.

In fact, he, President Kennedy, changed his plans with
his motorcade and was flown by helicopter everywhere he went
when he was there.

Before we can jump to any conclusions, which we have
not about the Milteer tape, it is significant that this fellow
who was involved in the most extreme and sordid heinous
type of right-wing activity would have made this kind of
a statement, actually predicting the manner in which the
President was killed, on November 9, 1963.

This tape was played the next day for FBI people and
Secret Service people. We have a photograph that was taken
by Mr. Augens of the AP wire service of the Presidential

SECRET

69   2-176

motorcade as it was approaching the plaza, making a left-hand

turn on Elm Street. There is a photograph of an individual

who looks again -//- I underscore this very much -//- like

Mr. Milteer.

Miss Hess went down to Milteer's residence in Georgia.

We had permission of the Judge down there, Judge Knight.

Milteer's estate was in probate. With his permission, we

were able to go through some of his belongings and property

and material.

She found a photograph of Milteer -//- this is not to

throw bouquets at us -//- but let me just note that in many

of the books that are written on the assassination, they

have a photograph of this Joseph J. Milteer. The photograph

is not a picture of Milteer, although they claim that it

is.

Miss Hess found this photograph -//- we had not been in

business that long -//- it is just an example of the kind of

research staff that we have. I have to doff my cap to her,

she has done a great job.

What we would like to do is compare through the use of

experts on a consultant basis and have them compare the

Milteer photo with the photo that we have of Milteer's

picture. If, indeed, Milteer is there watching the President,

one other coincidence when added to all of these other facts

that we certainly we would like to investiate.

70   SECRET   2-177

¶ Now, with regard to Milteer, when I say we would like
to investigate, Milteer is dead; nobody is going to point the
finger at Milteer. Obvously, we are not going to resurrect
him and bring him up here.

But the FBI interviewed Milteer on November 27, 1963.
They gave that report to the Warren Commission. They never
mentioned, from what we know of documentation about that
interview, that they had a tape of Milteer when they interviewed him and confronted Milteer with his own words on the
tape.

They merely interviewed Milteer the way they interviewed
thousands of other people, instead of pulling out the trump
card and asking him, "did you predict the manner in which
the President of the United States would be murdered," in fact
he denied it the play the tape for him, which would be
done in the ordinary course of a decent investigation.

That is not indicated in any material that the FBI has,
so there is no indication, because in the report that we have
in regard to the Milteer interview, there is nothing
mentioned. There is nothing to indicate that this tape was
ever brought to the attention of the Warren Commission.

I would ask you, Mr. Chairman, if you would use your
good offices to try to obtain for us the testimony that was
produced before the Schweiker committee. That, of course,
would be very helpful, as would all the documents relative

SECRET

These diagrams are from the 1979 HSCA Report, Volume VI, which contain discussions about whether the person in Dallas is indeed Milteer. That claim is dismissed on three factors: thickness of his lips, his hairline, but the biggest factor was his height. The committee experts estimated his height at 5' 10" +/-1" and had his height at 5' 4" or 5 '5". In 1963, I had estimated his height at 5' 8", as had earlier Secret Service reports.

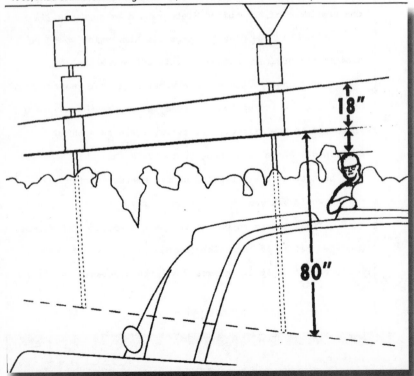

Index

Index